Redneck Spirituality

—Book Five—

*From the Depths of
Rumi's Outhouse*

<u>Authored as E. Egorhh Frank</u>

Redneck Spirituality—THE SERIES
Books One thru Five

Books One and Two Combined Edition—
(Print Form Only)

<u>Authored as Edmond E. Frank</u>

The Courage of a Butterfly—the novel
The Soul of an Eagle—the sequel
A Butterfly's Transformation in Poetry
An Eagle's Flight in Poetry

Redneck Spirituality

—Book Five—

From the Depths of Rumi's Outhouse

By
E. Egorhh Frank

Paperback ISBN 979-8-9854558-4-7

Dedication

Perceptions comprise our whole world. They are the product of what we choose to believe from what we are taught by those in authority. We were that child who then was just learning. When contaminated by the lies of our society, our perceptions can only be changed by accepting life's truths—and by our love.

Yet when led by our fears, our beliefs in the lies are often strong. And when compounded by our own personal fears, sometimes irresistible.

Back then, I was the lowest worm in both our family outhouses, a worm who now knows and accepts the truth of "what is." A worm you never knew during life, who still loves you, but never got to say goodbye.

I dedicate this book to my parents—

all four of them.

Acknowledgments

It appears there were few who wanted to put their fingers in this pumpkin pie. But hey, I love pumpkin pie, especially with whipped cream. But a pumpkin pie is made from everything but the shit inside a pumpkin.

While most self-help books resemble a pumpkin pie hidden beneath a covering of sweet whipped cream, this one does not. The back cover warning is for real.

Self-help is not about looking at the outside unblemished covering. Or about smothering everything in enough sweetness and light to uplift.

It is about looking at the personal shit inside you—the stuff that doesn't smell so good, the stuff that authors of this genre don't like to write about unless they can cover it with a disguise.

Therefore, when one of my critique groups demanded I not bring any more of this material—effectively censuring me—that was when I knew this had to be said. I meant the subtitle when I wrote it:

From the Depths of Rumi's Outhouse

So, to the few who helped me with this book, I owe you my deepest gratitude. This includes those in the critique group above. It is because of you that this book exists. Sincerely, THANK YOU.

To the Henderson Writers' Group, thanks for having my back and critiquing the writing, even though the content was something some clearly didn't want to deal with. The reality of this fractured world sometimes stinks, and you gotta know, that stink is all about our judgments . . . some of it yours, some mine. Still, I believe the only thing that reeks about it all is greed—the lust for power over one another. You, in the HWG are the ONLY critique group in town who refused to capitulate in giving a minority of Liberals the power to shut me up.

Thank you, Joyce Mochrie, my copy editor/proofreader and owner of *One Last Look,* for making space to edit this book.

onelastlookcopyedits.com

Your schedule was so busy that it looked like it would not happen before a quarter past never. I cannot say enough about the excellence of your work.

Then there were the three beta readers. I'm sorry that, in the end, I couldn't give you enough time. I do appreciate the efforts of those who came through with what they had: Ruthi L. Stucki, Dee Pluta, and Marilyn Crawley.

There is Karen Diehl, who would have stood in as editor had I given her time. Thank you, Karen.

Lastly, there is Bobby Daniels, my cover designer extraordinaire and owner of *Bobby Daniels Graphics.*

Bdanielsgraphics.com

He is a professional in the artistry of his work, even when dealing with the anality of my demands. He, too, I wholeheartedly recommend.

It was my choice to go ahead with publishing. I am sending all of you a proof copy as promised.

Epigraph

Spiritual Law #3: *Thoughts are energy.*

Truth is, *everything one creates in life begins as a thought.* As the sole creator of our lives, we choose, in every second of life, the energy with which we are creating. *It can only be one of two energies: the energy of all that is love, or the energy of all that is not love (fear).* The love you give to others comes from an abundance of love energy you have within you.

But what is the truth in this life? Most people spend the greater portion of it in the energy of fear and don't have much love energy to give others.

Most books about Spiritual Laws are written from the energy of love, pointing out the energy of your fear. The *Redneck Spirituality* series is different. It is written from the standpoint of truth. And yes, truth is, for the most part, we live our lives in the energy of fear while seeking the energy of love. *The energy of fear is always a cry for love.*

Coach Egorhh

Table of Contents

PART THREE—*Spirituality*

PART ONE
Introduction

This series is set up according to depth, the concepts in each higher-numbered book getting deeper. Welcome to the deep end of the spiritual pool of life.

Setting Up the Win

Want to change your life? That's what reading self-help books is all about, what this *Redneck Spirituality* series is about. But nobody wants to change their life if it works for them. So why are you reading this? What is it that doesn't work?

I'll simplify it in the most obnoxious of terms repeatedly. Here it is in a nutsack. *No matter how miserable one's life is, it is familiar—no threat. They know the score and are afraid to make changes. The threat is concerning the unknown, the change.*

Looking inside and using your *ability to respond* is the scariest of things ONLY because you know it will demand change. Most people won't look until their shitstorm of a life has hit the bottom of the cesspool, and they are drowning.

It's reeee-uul simple, folks. That happens when your soul has decided to hit your RESET BUTTON and is giving you one final chance.

For me, my chance occurred in a hospital ICU with the Grim Reaper staring me in the face. Will it happen differently for you? Will he wipe your shit in your face, as he did mine? It will be multiple times here in this book—the SAME shit, different hand. His is not so gentle.

This whole series has been doing this same thing in progressively deeper ways. My greatest wish is that you get the point—my WISH, not a DEMAND. My ego does not hang on your decision. This is YOUR life, YOUR decision.

Before that ICU, I lived a selfish life. My wife was pretty much the only person in it to whom I offered my love. But shit! What did I know about life or love . . . certainly not the good shit?

I know a lot more now. At times, this book series may come across as rude. Just know it is from my love that I bother to write about it.

Love. Real love? I loved my wife. She didn't love me back in the same way—the way I wanted it. That does not mean she didn't love me, nor did it define my own love.

Everyone who plays a part in your life has a lesson—
a gift for you.

My wife's lesson was perfect. You see, you don't have to accept, or RETURN, the love I offer in these books MY way. But love IS the gift offered here. Spiritual Law states: *The energy out, returns in kind.* But it doesn't have to come from you. *Love is a gift, and gifts don't require paybacks.*

One great truth of life is that it's about getting your soul's lessons. Significant others are perfect for rubbing those lessons in your face. I don't regret even one second of loving her. She taught me so much about me, and best of all, she taught me how to love.

Questions:
- What change DO you want? It's okay if you don't know right now. After all, this IS a self-help book, and knowing the answer to that question may be the help for which you are searching.
- And the question right now? Are you just going to READ this workbook, or are you going to DO it?

Action:
- These questions are about your intentions. After all, what self-help is all about is DOING not LOOKING. You might look at that now, before you begin.

Playing in Rumi's Field

This may be your first book of this series. I have attempted to lay it all out by book number as to the depth of the concepts presented. With this book, you are jumping into the deep end.

Just know that with self-help workbooks, there are two basic types of people: There are those who come to the game to sit in the bleachers above it all and enjoy themselves, and there are those who come to play, down here on the field of life.

Sometimes there are bumps and bruises, but any roughing up is done by you, for you. For purposes here, consider this field as Rumi's Field—a thirteenth-century Persian poet and Sufi mystic.

> *"Out beyond ideas of wrongdoing and*
>
> *rightdoing, there is a field. I'll meet you there."*
>
> *Rumi*

But you may be a third type who comes to the game and from the bleachers develops a yen to play in the game. It's your life. Do it your way.

If you intend to play, you will want a notebook in which to record your answers to the questions. Answer the questions and include any thoughts you may have about them. If more questions are then raised in your mind, write them down as well. Write only on the right-hand sheet.

After you have completed this book, go back and answer any questions you may have skipped. You can use the left-hand sheet for doing this.

As to the notebook? I suggest it be a loose-leaf type, something you can add pages to when later something strikes you. I don't expect, or want, you to just accept what is said here. I have only one hard-and-fast rule, and that is:

Do your own fucking thinking!

This last sentence is stressed purposefully for you, redneck style. If you took offense with my use of language, just know that there will occasionally be more to come.

The offense part? That will be a priceless eye-opener for you later. Taking offense does something to one's psyche that most people don't realize. Seeing something differently is what self-help is all about.

And speaking about seeing something differently . . . I will be offering up many of the Spiritual Laws for you to consider. All are simple truths of life and can be addressed with a short sentence or two, but there are only a few upon which I will concentrate. Those will be presented in different scenarios and repeated often.

Because they are deep, very few people will get them with only one pass or realize their depth. Bear with me on that. Here is one: *Your world is not "OUT THERE," rather, it is "IN HERE."*

And its depth? *Everything begins as a thought. Changing even one thought in your mind will change your whole life.*

This book is intended to plumb the depths of your life and to illuminate it with the light of truth. By that light, your life will look vastly different. You will see things you had no ability to see before. While the Spiritual Laws are about the simple truths of life, those truths are like an interlocked fabric. Some of the threads are identical in application, just a little different in color. In the three previous paragraphs, I used three different laws to illustrate my point.

In presenting it to you, you will find that *I repeat myself often.* Have you ever noticed that in commercials, something is often repeated—sometimes word for word, sometimes just slightly different in the circumstance or words used? The person marketing whatever doohickey being sold is trying to drum it into your head and/or make it personal to your life.

I repeat the same laws and concepts often. And yes, usually in different circumstances, applications, combinations, or even wording. Like that salesman, I am offering it up in different ways in an attempt to touch you in your life. Like an experiential seminar, I need to make a connection with your experiences for you to want to look.

This book is about self-help. It is written by and for rednecks. They are folks who give it to you straight, the reality as that redneck sees it. That's not to say it will be the same for you.

As the Spiritual Law states: *Your world "in here" is composed of how you see it—your perceptions and beliefs about everything.* Nobody's world is ever exactly the same.

For the most part, people expect books to be uplifting. That's especially true for self-help. But the truth about changing anything in your life is that you've got to look at all the shit you have never wanted to see . . . shit that is there, but ignored, no matter how badly it stinks up your life.

In looking at it, you will NEVER see it as uplifting—not until AFTER you have changed your thinking. That is the only way: *Change your perception, change your life.* If something is stinking up your life, you have to make it unacceptable and flush it.

PART TWO
The Spiritual Laws

The Spiritual Laws are simply the truths of life. As such they
have been reiterated by multiple writers, multiple times.
I do not claim them as my own intellectual property.

NOTE

If you are someone who is playing on the field of life, the laws pages in this section are something you will likely want to refer back to often.

In this part I have abbreviated the laws down to just the short version in order to help you find the one to which you need to refer.

I suggest you put a stick-on tab on the edge of the first page of each the short and long versions. The short version will have a page number referencing each law to its counterpart in the longer version.

The Spiritual Laws in Short

#50—What is of true evil in this life is created in the process of determining what is good and what is bad—and especially in what is right and wrong.

#51—This life—this part you play in God's experience of life—is your true destiny.

#52—You always have exactly what you want in life.

#53—How every religion perceives the afterlife —heaven—to be, is always the truth.

#54—In creating everything in life, love conquers all.

>>>End of Laws Listed in Book Four<<<

#55—The only reason you allow someone to be in your life is because they serve yours in some way.

#56—Sex is not love. It is an action that may be performed in the energy of love. It is a need. One that everyone has a need to do.

 # 57—There are no selfless acts. No one does anything whereby it does not benefit one's own self in some way.

#58—One's wants are governed by one's needs. Ultimately, one's needs are the needs —the lessons—of the soul.

#59— *The perceived value is equal to the conceived cost.*

#60—*Helping is really taking when it is saving others from doing something they have the ability to do for themselves.*

#61— *I am responsible for my feelings and will hold you capable and responsible for yours.*

#62—*Making someone else responsible for our happiness is never functional, Just as taking responsibility for their unhappiness is not also.*

#63—*When we don't accept the truth of "what Is," we guarantee ourselves pain.*

#64—*If it's in your face, it's either a lesson, a message, or a test from your soul, validating and acknowledging your learning.*

#65—*To show SYMPATHY for someone is to set yourself up as above—better than—them and serves only to lower the energy of both. EMPATHY is a gift you give that raises you both.*

#66—*The meeting of needs is the glue that holds a relationship together. Needs are the driving force behind every relationship. Love cannot suffice without meeting one another's fearful needs.*

Page—82

#67—*It can be more joyous to parent a child who is of your heart than one merely of your flesh.*

Page—82

#68—*Gratitude is our way of thanking that Higher Power. Gratitude raises one's energy beyond the natural evolution of one's soul.*

Page—83

#69—*The energy of fear is always a cry for love.*

Page—83

How's That Working for You?

So, okay. I've given you the short version of these Spiritual Laws. If you accept them, you'll find many more than just the ones I have listed. Remember, whatever holds true in this life is a Spiritual Law. Simple, hey? Looking by their light, you will see things about life that others simply can't, maybe because of what you will now know that they don't.

Yet in a world filled with lies—lies designed for one person to control others—those lies form the perception with which most in this world perceive life. They are the light by which life is generally showcased. And still, they are lies, the dysfunctions by which most find themselves crippled in life.

The Spiritual Laws, the simple truths, illuminate life differently, functionally, but very few ever grow spiritually enough to see by their light. For those who do, life is then something the others will never experience but all unknowingly want. Living life by the lies of others will always make one a victim.

So why discount the truth in favor of those lies? The truth has always been out there in everyone's face. Our soul inherently knows the truth. It spends your entire lifetime offering it up as lessons. The only benefit one will ever receive for not accepting those lessons is to abdicate one's responsibilities. We get to blame, but we never get to be in control of our own life.

How's that working for you?

I need to know that I am not just pissing into the wind. Give this book a review so others may know, too. It is usually fun to run in the rain, provided it IS rain.

If you are like most people, you **don't appreciate someone** telling YOU how THEY see life **differently from you. No** problem.

Like me, you will be looking to connect with those who see— or want to see—life's truths the same as I do. There are already

enough pissed off people in this **world just running around** pissing on one another's parade.

Questions:
- You can recognize someone who is just looking to piss on someone else's parade, can't you?
- Can you see that you might be tempted to have a pissing contest with them?

Action:
➢ DON'T.

The Spiritual Laws in Full

#1—*I am the Creator.*

Most only take this to mean I create my own life. That is true. But to own it requires an understanding that there is nothing in my life I have not had the deciding factor in creating. It is true, too, that all other Spiritual Laws presented here are just aspects of this one. As you read through and comprehend the concepts in this book, you will get a sense of how this Spiritual Law touches upon the infinite.

On a personal level, it refers to responsibility. What is your responsibility in life? It's much easier to see this by simply looking at what the meaning is of that word. From the roots out, it means ability to respond. That is from where one must look to determine their responsibility in anything.

If you do something in your life that someone else takes offense to and harbors hard feelings toward you—yes, you did the act. But did you choose those feelings the other person feels? No, but you always have a responsibility to your intentions. Did you intend for them to be pissed at you before you did the deed?

If so, then you do bear the responsibility of intentionally trying to manipulate them in their life. You just broke a different law that hasn't yet been mentioned. This is what is meant by "other aspects of this law."

Questions:

- Do you see why it is that your responsibility in life revolves *only* around those areas where you have an ability to respond?

- Do you realize that you *always* have an ability to respond to how you choose to think about and to feel about *everything*?

Actions:

➤ Again, like all the other books in this series, this is a workbook. And as mentioned, to do the work, you will need a separate notebook. Make your heading on the first page, "DO YOUR OWN THINKING." You might want to make it so throughout your notebook. It is critically important. (Feel free to add an F-bomb for emphasis.)

➤ In the past, many have attempted to use these laws with the intention of manipulating other people's feelings. Just knowing these truths gives you an advantage in your life that most don't have. *You* will always have the "responsibility of your intentions" to always use these laws with loving intent. List the laws *you* would be breaking in manipulating other people's feelings (there are more than one). You will need to recognize them all by yourself when we come to them, then come back to list them in your notebook here, so leave room. This will be your first exercise in doing your own thinking.

➤ Let's look at those lies society has taught us to believe. With the truth of every law that you will come across here, society will likely have a counter lie. In fact, make a special section titled "Society's Lies." Leave plenty of room.

To get you started, I will gift you with society's lie for the first law: *I am the Creator.*

Society's Lie:
Creator? YOU don't create your life. Shit happens, and other people do stuff to you. *Now you take it from here.*

#2—*Thoughts create.*

Look around you. Everything our species ever created began as a thought in someone's mind. As for the rest, there is an order to the Universe, one that speaks of a sentience—to feeling, sensing, understanding, creating—like us, but much more. It is that *Higher Power*, infinitely beyond what our religions can conceive.

This law can also be stated: *Everything begins as a thought. Change your mind, change your life.*

Questions:

- Change is about being pushed away from something and/or being pulled toward something else. Those "somethings" are thoughts—conscious ones to be effectively controlled.
- What do you need to change, to see something differently?
- What are the things in your thinking that you are willing to change?
- So far, what lies have you discovered that led your life to be dysfunctional?
- Are you angry about those lies—at those who told them to you?
- Be angry, yes, but at whom? Most of your teachers were taught by someone before who was also an innocent child when they, too, were taught. Do you understand that the original asshole who knew the truth—and the few who learned it later—only wanted to control?
- It is ONLY the lie you see now that deserves your anger because the assholes who knew the truth then are likely dead, lost to you in the mists of time. What

would be the lie that society tells concerning this law?

Actions:

- ➢ Make a list of things in life that you don't like.
- ➢ List those you want to change. Do they pull you toward or push you away from? Your choice of feelings is what determines it—key word "choice."
- ➢ Do you understand that your feelings are the key to changing things in your life?
- ➢ You have virtually no control over what others do. Or how when thinking as a victim, life comes to you. More on that later. But feelings are a choice and can be changed. It is easier to do if you can recognize what the benefit is in something you don't like. Everything you have in life has some benefit for you, or you would not have created it being there. You will need to see how silly some of those benefits are if you want to change anything.
- ➢ So what benefit is there in believing those controlling lies of Society? I'll give you this one. Responsibility. As a victim you don't have to take responsibility for anything. You get to blame that on others or circumstances—BIG WHOOP ON THAT. List everything you don't like in your life and then list what possible benefit it could have. Hint: for most it will be this same one.

>>><<<

#3—*Thoughts are energy.*

In being our own Creator, we choose, in every second of life, the energy with which we are creating. It can only be *one* of *two* energies—the energy of *all that is love*, or the energy of *all that is not love* (fear).

Both are contagious, and both infect those close by. One acts as a disease, the other, the cure. When it comes to the energy, there are many diseases, but there is only the one cure.

Out beyond these two energies, there is a third state of being. *This state exists in the space of no energy and is called "don't give a shit"—a state of indifference. It is the opposite of both love and fear. It creates NOTHING.*

Question:
- Do you see that as everything begins as a thought, then everything we create in life is created in the energy of love or fear? **(THIS LAW HOLDS THE KEY TO YOUR HAPPINESS.)**

Actions:
- ➢ What would be a lie that society tells us about this law? Can you think of more?
- ➢ On a separate sheet of paper, list some things that you have happening, or that have happened lately, that you have strong feelings about. Then label them as created in the energy of love or fear. (It is either/or. The two energies can **never** exist together.)
- ➢ Now transfer them to your notebook under those two labels.
- ➢ For those labeled "FEAR," list the most fucked-up ones first.
- ➢ List those under "LOVE" with the most joyful ones first.
- ➢ Which of those under "FEAR" will you begin changing first?
- ➢ As fearful thoughts are almost always about things that have not happened, and likely never will, worrying about them is a waste. Will you let go of the worry?
- ➢ You do know that this will be a shitload of fear that you will be flushing?
- ➢ And do you know that you cannot exist in the energy of love if you are already in the energy of fear? Hard to change if you have no experience in love. Make that your first priority.

>>><<<

#4—*The energy out returns in kind.*

The energy of your every thought determines what comes to you in life—*love* or *fear*. This is that freedom of choice, which is our greatest gift of all creation. It is this choice that creates the path of our lives and the quality with which we walk.

Vulnerability. For most, it is a fearful thing. It is this fear with which many choose to live their lives—at war, always in fearful attack, or warding off, protecting with equally fearful energy. Fear serves to ward off love every time. If you are alone in life, look at that one. Those who have come to know the Spiritual Laws seldom live in the energy of fear.

And yet, it is a choice, like integrity is also a choice. (We will talk about that later—Law #11.) I mention it here because love, like integrity, is something we have all been trained not to show to the world.

The lie society would have us believe is that to do so makes us vulnerable. Truth is, if we don't give love, we don't get love, just as this law states.

The issue of integrity and society is simply that society would have us wear a façade—that showing up naked, as who we are, is also a vulnerable thing. And without your façade, to show you as being who they want, you will not be accepted. Doesn't that suggest that those in society, as a whole, are phony assholes? (No pun intended.)

And in the reality of life, love and integrity are things we aspire to always have, but not always do. Sometimes we slip in life and must recalibrate ourselves. This is one aspect of being conscious.

Questions:
- Are you beginning to see the lies society demands we believe?

- Who, or what, are you really vulnerable to? Do you see that being "vulnerable" has physical aspects?
- What about the mental aspects (for you) of being vulnerable to the thoughts of others?
- Are those mental thoughts, which are the most destructive, your thoughts about you or their thoughts about you—the ones that you believe are true? Are they?

Actions:

➢ Write about any lies our society uses to counter this law. ***Make this the FIRST thing you determine and make note of with each law.*** I don't want to be repeating this every time, but likely will.

➢ What are the physical aspects of being vulnerable? Write about them.

➢ Write about how vulnerability affects you in how others perceive you.

➢ Write about how their perceptions affect you physically.

➢ How do their mental thoughts affect you? Write about it.

➢ Do you think it is possible to be your authentic self if you are worried about what they think of you? Write about it.

➢ It is a choice you have in your face right NOW—to run your life according to how YOU feel about you, or to be controlled by how THEY feel about you.

➢ Where does your ability to respond lie? With your feelings or theirs? Choose!

>>><<<

#5—*The Universe always balances.*

With every sorrowful thing, there is the potential for an equal joy, yet we are the Creators in our lives. **There is equal joy to be found in every sorrowful event if we will look for it and accept it. We will receive it whether we do so consciously or not. In the duality of this life, you have already paid the price. It can also be said as:** *For every fearful thing that happens, there is a gift of wonder, equal in magnitude.*

Just so, from the opposite end, *for every joyful thing one receives, there is a price to be paid.* Again, the Universe always balances. There are no free lunches.

It might also be said: *The greater the wounding, the more magnificent can be the healing.*

This is one law we would all be wise in knowing the reaches of, but few do. This is why I told it to you in four different ways. The truth is, it was we who chose the sorrow, and it is we who must seek and choose the joy. The potential for both exists in balance within the Universe. When we are open to it, we are but a shift of mind away, requiring no more struggle than the acceptance of our next breath.

Questions:

- Can you see why knowing that we are the Creator of our life **denies us the ability to believe the lie of blame?**
- **Do you now realize that we are also denied our victimhood in life**—other people have no power over our feelings except what we give to them?
- Do you realize that these two things, now denied us, have set us free?
- Society cannot control your life without you believing these lies. Can you wrap your mind around that one?
- The mantle of a responsible Creator may seem more difficult to bear. You can take heart in your newly won freedom.
- It always takes time dealing with the shit in one's life before one starts to look for and see the joyful reflections arising out of it. In the beginning, those things usually sneak up on you.

Actions:

- Now write down the date when you feel you have a handle on it and responsibility just "feels right."
- Note down and date any further slips (there will be some). You have been trained in the lies for how many years?

- ➤ At some point, blaming and denying responsibility will become a disgusting thing to you. Note down the date and write about it.
- ➤ Write about the joy that has been fertilized and has grown out of the shit. The joy won't stop showing up—don't stop writing about it. Nothing is ever concluded until you have taken it to gratitude.
- ➤ Now, see to it that when your whole life ends, it is in gratitude.

>>><<<

#6—*The energy of thoughts must flow.*

Once taken in, the energy of fear stays and is the initial cause of all sickness *if* it is not felt, acknowledged, and then released.

Even love energy must be released—given back out—in order to flow.

With Law #3, we talked about the two basic types of energy: LOVE and everything that is not love (FEAR). Now we talk about the energy of fear and how it leads to disease (dis-ease). Most people never realize it, but once you understand about the two energies, can there be any denying that point?

So now, what about the energy of love and how it differs from fear? Sometimes others see unintended fearfulness in your interaction, but they are the ones creating their own fear. But what about love? Love is a gift that may or may not be accepted.

You see, once given, it is theirs to do with as they please. Some will accept it, some won't. Our only part in it is to give it. Once given, there cannot be any strings attached, no demands on it being returned, no expectations on what that other person does with it. Otherwise, it was never a gift of love, but only a bribe.

Even you just wanting it to be returned is a denial that it was ever love. Loving someone who doesn't return it can be the greatest gift you can receive. By you simply giving the gift of it without stopping is to know your capacity to truly love.

It is a sure thing to believe you love someone, but you get to know the truth about it when it is not returned. Will you have the ability to accept that fact and still love? If not, do you see the expectations attached?

I tell you this from experience. I was married to my first wife for over twenty-five years. We only divorced because the marriage no longer worked. The truth about relationships is that of meeting one another's needs. Loving her was one of my needs. Hers were different, and I found myself unable to meet them.

I was her security, never her love. Funny thing . . . the energy of fear ages and causes dis-ease. I'm seventy-two and look to be twenty years younger. I still love her and expect that I will even beyond my death.

That has not stopped me from letting go of her and loving another. The picture on this cover is me at seventy-two years old. I believe it was all that love flowing through me that served to keep me looking so young. We are not meant to be vessels for holding energy. We are more like conduits for directing it. Energy? Everything is energy. The issue is what you will do with the energy coming into your life.

Questions:
- Do you accept the love of others?
- Do you return it? If so, is it in the way they want it?
- Do they accept it in the way you give it? If not, then is it possible it wasn't love but rather a bribe? Seeing that, can you still love them?
- Do you have certain people in your life whom you love?

- Do you have any pets—animals that you love?
- Things—possessions or toys. You may find joy in such things, but can you see that isn't love?
- Is there someone whom you love but who doesn't love you in return? Do you accept that and love them even so?

Actions:

➢ Make a list of everything and everyone in your life that you love.

➢ List everything and everyone you hate or that you are angry with.

➢ Which list serves to suck you dry, pull you down? Which raises you up?

➢ Everything in your life has a purpose that serves you in some way. Those things that suck you dry serve you somehow. Figure it out and write it down.

➢ Then ask yourself if the price is too steep.

➢ Put a roll of toilet paper next to the shitter and list those things on the sheets.

➢ Now use that toilet paper for what it was intended for and give it a one-fingered salute as you flush that crap out of your life.

➢ It's okay if you have a few cling-ons. You've put the question into your subconscious, and eventually, it will give up the answers. You can then finish the process.

>>><<<

#7—*Along with being the Creator comes responsibility. One cannot BE the Creator and play the blame game.*

One cannot *"not"* create. Each person must accept responsibility for the totality of creating his or her life, especially for all thoughts and feelings associated in that process.

Blame is the abdication of responsibility, the greatest of all of mankind's dysfunctional lies. Responsibility—the ability to respond—is what just IS. It is integral to you and cannot be given away.

Most people create their lives unconsciously. Things happen and they react. Few people actually act with any thought or consideration behind that act. This does not mean that you are not responsible for your actions, nor does it negate that you created what comes next in your life.

But what about your feelings? How many people do you think actually choose how they want to feel about things . . . consciously make that determination?

Are you getting that while it may be created unconsciously, you are still the Creator and you are *always* creating? Trying to abdicate that responsibility with blame is always a lie.

Questions:
- That lie of blame—who or what do you think is the ultimate authority in the matter?
- Are you telling that lie to other people or to yourself? Or are you telling it to everyone, including yourself?
- But *everyone* is *not* the ultimate authority. *You* are, or perhaps more accurately, your soul is. Do you see that? *Your soul* knows if you are lying.
- Do you see that blame is one of society's nastiest lies?
- Do you see that by denying responsibility, you have given up all your power in life?
- Know what that makes you? Try this: a flaming, fucking victim.

Action:
- Obviously, blame is the current lie for this law. Where else—how else—do you not take responsibility in creating your life? List those things down. Do you have a list?
- Now in honesty, is there anything there that does NOT involve blame?

>>><<<

#8—*The world is not "out there"—it's "in here."*

It is comprised of every thought, every belief, and every feeling you have. Your world is totally your responsibility because you are the only one who has the ability to respond— the ability to make it better or worse, loving or fearful. Only you can change your mind.

Look at *Law #2—Thoughts create*. Do you see the connection? These laws are very much the supporting, interlocking fabric of life.

No one else lives in exactly the same world as you. Those whose worlds are close, similar to yours, will be the ones drawn to you. And often, it will be others whose worlds are not close but who will see yours and want it for themselves. You may help them by being true to yourself.

This can never happen unless they see who you are, understand how you think, and then accept it for themselves. It is always a process of attraction, them wanting to think like you. Changing anything in their life must be done by themselves, through *want*, not by you, through your *will*.

Questions:
- This isn't "The" World or even "My" World, but "Your" World. Do you get that?
- Can you see why my world is not the same as yours?

Actions:

> ➤ Next time you're tempted to tell someone that they're wrong, say instead: "We—you and I—don't live in the same world."
> ➤ If you can handle it, you might preface that with "You're right."

#9—*Others are but a mirror for us to see ourselves.*

What we don't like in others is but the reflection of what we don't like in ourselves. If it were not also within us, we could never see it in them.

Question:

> • Can you see how society lies about this? That others are at fault—the **BLAME** game?

Action:

> ➤ A lot of people are so steeped in this lie that they can't understand what this law is saying. Can you? Write about it.

#10—*The purpose of life is for those lessons.*

It is our soul's job to supply the lessons. When we refuse the learning, the lessons will be presented again, more forcefully, until we learn them—or die.

This law is the reason I took that "Road Less Traveled"—why I came to find myself in an ICU expecting to die. Yes, my soul had a lot to teach me and is why I write these books. I was very aware his finger was on my reset button.

Questions:

> • Do you understand?
> • Do you agree? Disagree?

Actions:

> ➤ Again, what lies does society tell you about this? Write.

> ➢ Write down your thoughts on this. Come back to them after you have finished this book.
> ➢ If you find they've changed, write about how and why.

>>><<<

#11—*Self-esteem requires integrity. It is the respect of your soul.*

What our heart feels—and what we think, say, and do—must all align as the same. And all must be coupled with the strength of intention to be in integrity. Integrity commands esteem, both in ourselves and from others.

Question:
- Most folks have never heard it defined this way. Have you?

Actions:
> ➢ How have you heard it defined?
> ➢ Or if not, how have you been defining it? Write.

>>><<<

#12—*Our lives are run primarily by our needs, then by our wants.*

As such, our lives are mostly run from an unconscious level. We all know what it is we want, but few know what we need to have it. Needs are about the necesssities of life. Wants are about the quality of life.

Questions:
- Do you understand that needs are run more by and for your soul? That if you aren't conscious of them, then it is only your soul that can be?
- Society's lies usually blame others for what you don't have. Do you find this to be so?
- Do you understand that there is a difference between needs and wants? In this asking, have you become aware of any needs you didn't know about consciously?

Actions:
- ➤ Make a list of all the needs you are aware of.
- ➤ List your wants.
- ➤ How many of the wants are dependent on your unmet needs?
- ➤ Are there any that you just now are becoming aware of? Write.

#13—*Our life is our sole possession—and so it is for everyone.* Another way of stating this is: ***Everyone is the Creator of their own life—and only their own***.

I cannot save another from, nor is it my birthright to interrupt, the process of another's learning. I may share my own learning, *if asked*, but it is only within my own mind that I can place correction. I have no control over another's.

And now, because this law is very much responsible for us getting our own shorts in a pinch, I'll repeat it a third time. *We, being the Creator, have all the say in creating our own life, but no say in the creation of anyone else's.* They are always free to be, say, or do whatever they want. The energy in which they do it—love or not—generally determines whether or not they stay in our life.

Questions:
- • When was the last time you stuck your nose in someone else's business without being asked?
- • How'd that work out for you?
- • When was the last time someone else stuck their nose in your business, unasked?
- • How'd that work for you? For them?

Action:
- ➤ Write about it, but try to limit it to the most important incidents. You have a book to read.

#14—*Change is the constant of the Universe.*

Change is fearful. With everything we find fearful, change—the unknown—will be at its core.

But fear? Fear is *not* a constant, it is a *choice* (Law #3). And sometimes, it is the barometer that indicates a need for change.

When you love someone and fear losing them from your life, the irony is definitely there—fear and love energies never mix, remember? If you don't grow together, you can only grow apart. You cannot avoid growing.

Questions:
- Do you get just how important it is to know which energy you are operating your life in—in every moment of it?
- You have control of it simply by your awareness—and by the courage of your choice. Can you see that?
- Honesty, integrity, courage, choosing love—all of it needs to match for a relationship to be functional. Do you see that?
- If you live your life in the energy of love, but they concentrate theirs on fear, do you think you will ever grow together?

Actions:
- ➤ Are you both on the same page with all this? Write down where you need to work on it together.
- ➤ If you have a significant other, I repeat: If you don't grow together, you can only grow apart. You cannot avoid growing. Your growth will be the reason you part.
- ➤ You grow together . . . or you grow apart. Either way, do it with love.

#15—*To create a functional life requires one to do one's own thinking.*

The beliefs passed down through the generations, as well as by our religions, are generally accepted as truth. Even when those "truths" serve us falsely, few have the courage to think for themselves. It takes great courage to think differently in the face of family and/or religion. Dysfunction always results from living a lie—any lie—your own or one passed down to you by others.

Question:
- Now, get clear. Can you understand why I keep harping on society's lies?

Actions:
- As you pass through this book, every time you see that your beliefs are crosswise to these Spiritual Laws, write it down.
- Make a special note of those crosswise beliefs you want to keep. Refer back to them at the end of this book. Those you still want to hang on to, write down how they serve you in life.

>>><<<

#16—*Controlling anyone outside ourselves is a fallacy.*

We can only control another inasmuch as they will let us—or rather, pretend to let us.

And feelings? We cannot control another's feelings any more than they can make us feel anything we don't choose to feel.

As for our world? See Law #8. Yes, we control our own world because it lies within us. And sometimes, if our connection to the source—to that Higher Power—is strong enough, our world then affects everyone's.

Questions:
- ➢ Are you getting an understanding about how this game of control is a farce?
- How it is a game that takes up the greatest part of everyone's life?
- Do you see the agonizing waste of it all?
- Do you see that it takes at least two to play this game?
- When will you stop playing?

Action:
- ➢ Make that your choice in every reclaimed moment of your life.

>>>END OF LAWS COVERED IN BOOK ONE<<<

#17—*The energy to which we hold fast is what runs our life.*

Mostly, it happens on an unconscious level. This is why, on the conscious level, forgiveness is so important to our souls. Forgiveness means to let go of any energy we hold toward others that drags our own energy down.

Questions:
- Society says that forgiving someone their transgression against you is a magnanimous thing to do. The lie is that your forgiveness is about them. Do you see that?
- Can you see that you are doing it for yourself—to free yourself of the burden of letting them control your future through your feelings?
- Whatever they did, you can be sure that, at that time, they were making themselves "right" about it in their minds. Regardless, your forgiveness releases you from the struggle. It also allows you to walk away, consciously knowing you are no longer a victim. Do you see that forgiving is simply saying, "I no longer give a shit about you and what you did?"

- If you can't say that, then you haven't truly forgiven yourself for your part of being a victim in their war. Do you see that?

Actions:

➤ Every war requires two or more people. Are you still one of them, being that you still give a shit—or do you? Write about it.

➤ Can you see the responsibility you admit to when you forgive?

➤ Remember Law #3—the *two* energies, love and fear? What this law doesn't mention is the third choice is no energy at all, as in, "Don't give a shit." Isn't that the truth about forgiveness?

➤ Obviously, if you're holding bad feelings, you clearly haven't forgiven. And can anyone this side of Mother Teresa sincerely say they love them? Maybe you can, but the only alternative is for you to love you enough to not give a shit about their fear. Let go of your feeling toward them and accept their right to be who they are. Write about it.

➤ "Don't give a shit" might actually clear the way for you to love again. You weren't loving anyone when holding that energy.

>>><<<

#18—*Soul-to-soul pacts are made in the pre-existence. Everyone participating in our lives is there by prior agreement. As such, they bear you a gift of learning.*

Each agrees to provide the lessons in life the other needs for the growth of his or her soul. Those people in your life who it seemed were especially mean—maybe you asked them to be. Or maybe it was about a lesson you are to provide them, one that required it to be so?

Just because the lesson does not feel so good does not mean your soul did not set it up to be exactly so. Those lessons that are the most painful are the ones that offer us the greatest learning. Our souls know it all already but need to experience it to truly "know." It is about that eighteen-inch journey between the head and the heart—or maybe between your consciousness and your soul. Despite what the ladies say about thinking with your "little head," your heart is where your soul resides.

Being a victim is not about the things that happen or what others do. The anger you experience from it simply says that in that fear-filled state of mind, you are being disloyal to yourself, to your soul.

But some hold on to that anger and use it to hide its true responsibility from themselves. Much easier to blame someone or something outside themselves and to be a victim. Being a *victim* is not about the things that happen or what others say or do. *It is always a state of mind—your mind.*

We, every one of us, have been taught to see ourselves as victims—by society, our religions, our spouses, our relatives, and even our friends.

It is about control and about blame. Hell, it's about a shitload of those lies we've been taught to see as the truth of life.

Because everyone does set these things up before coming into life, not even children can be honest victims. The experience of being helplessly victimized was needed for my soul's growth.

As an adult, I now know why—*I could not have grown past being a victim without actually becoming one.* Who, but a helpless child, can better experience being a victim? The question then becomes: When will one stop being a victim?

Questions:
- I've written two novels based on the story of my life— *The Courage of a Butterfly* and *The Soul of an Eagle*. In both, I've taken the concept of this law as having made such a pact with the Angel of Death, a character who liked to be called Big D. Having found myself in an ICU, fully expecting to die . . . maybe that is not just a concept, but the truth. Has anyone reading this ever known such an experience? If so, I suspect that although Big D is a fictional character in the stories, he is maybe not so much so in my life—or yours.
- Enough with the promoting. Did you ever meet a stranger you felt heavily drawn toward, like you already knew them?
- Did any such person fail to play an important part in your life? Think about it.

Action:
➤ Write about him/her/them.

>>><<<

#19—*We are, quintessentially, beings of energy.*

Our energy affects that of the others around us. We cannot avoid it and are always attracted to those of like energy.

Everything is energy in one form or another. While energy can and does change forms, it cannot be destroyed.

The energy that comprises our physical bodies . . . it's clear how that changes. It is the energy that is our higher self—our soul—that concerns us the most. But remember, energy cannot be destroyed. Isn't that saying there is an afterlife?

Questions:
- Have you ever known a psychic vampire, someone who, when they are around you, just sucks your energy dry?
- Do you know anyone who uplifts your energy and is a joy to be around?

Actions:
- ➢ Which type of person do you want to be? You'd think it would be a no-brainer. Choose!
- ➢ Make a list of everyone in your circle of friends. Put either a "V" (for vampire) or a "J" (for joy) next to each name.
- ➢ You might consider whittling the Vs out of your life.
- ➢ You will find that easy, unless your own name on their list would also have a "V" next to it. Like energy attracts like. Most likely, you will want to think deeply on this one. Write.

#20—*God, the Creator—that Higher Power infuses the energy of the entire Universe.*

We are part of that energy. We are each a part and piece of God. If God is within us, we MUST also be within God.

Questions:
- • Do you find it interesting that this law flies in the face of most organized Christian religions?
- • They teach that God is a being who looks like us and who lives in a place called heaven, a place apart and away from us. And that you need to go to that church to commune with Him/Her/It. Hmmmm?
- • And yet, doesn't the Bible, which they say is God's word, allude, in multiple places, to exactly what this law states?

Actions:
- ➢ I'm not saying the churches are wrong. I'm just asking you to consider another Spiritual Law that you haven't heard here yet: ***Perception is a choice***. We only see what we want to see, and we have to be "right." Write about that.
- ➢ Why do you suppose Organized Religions would want you to depend on them for your spiritual sustenance? Yup—write.

#21—*Real love, once given, cannot be taken back.*

There are all kinds of interactions that are generally billed as "love"—lust, caring, companionship, even ownership. All that mislabeling notwithstanding, "real love" is an all-or-nothing gift, given without exceptions, expectations, or demands for anything in return.

Real love begins with loving yourself. The love you hold within you—for you—*is* the love you give to another.

We have all been taught to control those around us, especially those we are close to. In fact, many see that age-old struggle to control as actually being love—US saving THEM from folly because we know better than they do. But control is fear, not love.

Why is it that when such a marriage fails, it generally results in hard feelings? Is it because they have lost control? Or maybe because they never loved each other at all?

Questions:
- Have YOU ever broken up in a relationship and had harsh feelings or been combative with one another?
- That would be fear energy, don't cha think?
- How long do you think fear was running that relationship?
- Was there ever time for love?

Actions:
- Look, you can't change the past.
- But you can stop the war now.
- Refusing to continue the fight—that's something you can do to start respecting yourself now.
- Loving yourself begins with respecting yourself.
- Right after that, respect turns to liking—then love. Yup, keep writing in your book. Maybe you, too, will publish it someday.

>>><<<

#22—*We can only feel our own feelings on a conscious level.*

The feelings, the energy of others, is felt at the soul level—our higher unconscious part. Our soul comprises the total energy of our being, most of which is beyond the conscious.

On this conscious level, you can only feel yourself loving them. Your love for another is a gift you give to you. If you expect it to be returned by them, then it was never a gift—it was never love. Gifts are given without expectations or payback.

And yet in this life, how many give their love without the expectation of it being paid back? Kind of a "Slick Willy" sales job, don't cha think?

Questions:
- Is it possible that loving someone is the most important part of a relationship?
- Far more satisfying than being loved back?
- If that isn't so for you, do you think maybe your love for them is really your fearful need to be loved?

Action:
- ➢ Write.

>>><<<

#23—*All life happens right now. Now is the only time there is for the living.*

The past is dead, and the future belongs to our dreams. We have only "the now!"

This is a no-brainer. You can't change the past. Yet how many people spend the bulk of their lives living in the "if onlys" or the "what ifs" of then?

And how much time do people spend worrying about the future? If you stop and think about it, most of those things you feared would happen never did.

Meanwhile, most of the time was spent in the energy of fear instead of the energy of love.

Questions:
- How often have you heard this one said?
- What, if anything, have you done about it?
- Do you live your life in joyful abandon—maybe like the child you once were likely did?
- Do you think you can recapture that childlike quality in your life again? You know, the wonder of all things new, the joy, the passion . . . the love?

Action:
- ➤ Do it!

>>><<<

#24—*Whatever our thoughts dwell upon with energy is what we are attracting into our lives right now.*

It's simply how we use our energy in the creation of our lives. Being actually a part of God (Law #20), we, too, hold the power. Few realize it is an ongoing process. We are constantly using that power in the creation of our lives. With it, you can create your fondest dream or your worst nightmare. Some call this "The Law of Attraction."

When using this law, one needs to remember the energy doesn't distinguish between what you don't want as opposed to what you do. It only knows what you concentrate your energy on and serves that up to you.

Focus your thoughts on your dreams, not your nightmares.

Questions:

- Did you ever see the movie *The Secret*?
- If so, what did you think of it?

Actions:

- ➢ If not, go see it. And then—you've got it—write about it.
- ➢ Also watch another movie called *The Moses Code*.
- ➢ Write about it, too.

>>><<<

#25—*Your every word is an order to your soul.*

Thoughts create, and if you don't want them manifested into your life, then that thought, and especially every thought once spoken, must be consciously cancelled—*with passion.*

That Higher Power we are all a part of does not differentiate between what we want and what we don't want. It only sees what we feel passionate about and brings that into being in our lives.

I'm talking passionate about—not horny. Although, that has always worked for me, too.

Questions:

- Can you see how this is Law #2 restated, looked at from a different angle?
- Why? Why do you think that is?
- How about Law #24, the one before this one?

Actions:

- ➢ It is always best to verbalize any cancellations out loud.
- ➢ You will find that a lot of folks will regard this as an apology.
- ➢ Whether said aloud or silently, it needs to be done immediately. Don't give yourself the time to create what you don't want in your life.

>>><<<

#26—*Change requires truth.*

Your thinking creates your life (Law #2). Change your mind, change your life. However, one cannot change anything about one's thinking unless it is the truth about what their heart wants. Pretending to accept someone else's thinking is to live a pretend life—never sustainable, always dysfunctional.

But then, that's about lying to others. How does one lie to one's self? YOU are the ONLY authority about YOU. Lying to yourself? How fucking dysfunctional do you need to be to believe those lies?

And yet, do you think there is a person alive who has not tried? Yes, we ALL do crazy shit when we won't accept the truth of "what is."

Questions:
- Have you ever told a lie only to find yourself drawn into a web?
- How each added lie in support of that original lie just drew that web in tighter until you couldn't remember the truth?
- Did the fabric of that web eventually collapse—or strangle you?
- Can you see that lies, by their very nature, are not sustainable?

Action:
- ➢ A promise to change something about yourself that you don't want to change is the same as a lie to your soul—again, not sustainable. Write about your own experiences.

>>>END OF LAWS COVERED IN BOOK TWO<<<

#27—*Life—all of it—is a spiritual experience.*

There is no part of life where God is not present, experiencing life with you. You are the vehicle by which God experiences life. As part of God, your soul knows everything, but just as it is in this life, knowing something in your head is not the same as knowing it in your heart. That takes experiencing. Your life gives your soul the experiences it needs, and ALL OF IT is for God to experience life—the great soap opera of life where God experiences all parts.

Do we provide that Higher Power with more than entertainment and amusement? I seriously don't know. Maybe I'm looking at it ass-backward. We are all part of the sentience behind the Universe. Do we serve God or does God serve us? Or is it a symbiotic relationship? We are certainly more than parasites. Parasites take and give the host back nothing.

I gotta say that we are of the utmost value. Why else would that Higher Power be so fixated on creating life in the bowels of this eternal Universe? We gotta mean more than just shit that has nurtured.

I wonder if we are even capable of knowing the answer to it all?

Question:
- Do you accept yet that these laws are the truths in life?

Actions:
- ➤ Are the nasty, mean, and foul things of life included as being "spiritual"? Write.
- ➤ "ALL OF IT is for God to experience life." CONFUSED? It will be explained more fully soon. Watch for it.
- ➤ So, it's okay if you don't know. Just come back here and write about it when you do.

#28—*Those times when life is at its most chaotic are the times of most opportunity.*

Change happens most often during those times because that very chaos gives you the reason to make that change in your thinking.

Living according to what is the truth lends functionality and calmness to your life, assuming you are mature enough to accept "what is."

Not accepting the truth of what is—the truth of the Spiritual Laws—therein lies the chaos that requires a rethinking.

Questions:
- Has there ever been a time of chaos in your life that didn't bring change?
- If so, what was the opportunity that you missed out on?
- Do you regret it?
- Or did you just not see it?

Actions:
- ➢ Change is the most frightening thing there is in this life. Not knowing who you'll become or how your life will be different is always frightening. And fear is not a thing of love, remember? Try facing the next change in your life with love—and courage.
- ➢ The next time your life becomes chaotic, face that with joyful anticipation. That would be about the energy of love, y'know?
- ➢ As always, write.

#29—*Your soul is you—from the lowest to the highest of the energy of you.*

From the autopilot of our lowest unconscious self, to the conscious and beyond, to the God-part of our highest self that touches all, that soul part is not a separate being. Its lessons are always for its—for our—highest good.

We are beings of energy inhabiting this physical body. Very little energy is required to run this body, and even less to run this consciousness. Most of that energy resides beyond what our consciousness can handle.

The faith of a mustard seed? If we truly knew who and what we are, we could play that game. You know, we could call it Mountain Moving, or Mountain Building, or just blowing shit up.

Questions:
- Are you now aware of your two choices of energy?
- Can you trust yourself, your soul, your God that in choosing love, the very best of life will come to you?

Actions:
- In the lies that society tells, is it any mystery that society wants you to regard yourself, your soul, and your God as separate beings? Elaborate more on that.
- Read and consider Law #4 again.
- Which energy will you be choosing to live with in life?
- Write about that.

>>><<<

#30—*Your soul is God, essentially made of the enigmatic substance of God. YOU are essentially a part of God, as are we all.*

God is infinite, and our physical self hasn't the ability to know infinity—or that aspect of God—other than through glimpses of it inside ourselves. God is everywhere and everything, but seeing God begins by looking within.

Questions:
- Does this law feel familiar?
- Yes? No? Maybe?

Actions:
> Read the next law. Then come back and write about what you think I'm doing.
> Is it working? Write.

>>><<<

#31—*You are physically of God—a drop in the ocean of God—a part of and the essence of it all.*

Like DNA carries all aspects of our physical self within each of our cells, our soul carries all the aspects of God within it. And we are our soul, remember? Perhaps the thirteenth-century Persian poet, Rumi, said it better: *"You are not a drop in the ocean, you are the entire ocean in a drop."* God is physically the whole of it all, and we are physically a part of God.

This Law is a repeat of *Law #30*, as is *Law #20*. Given how religions have tried to separate us from God, this concept is especially hard for people to understand. Many New Thought writers leave this one out, or downplay it, perhaps thinking that you will come to this realization on your own.

But then, I'm a redneck, and even I had it listed as separate laws UNTIL NOW. This law is just that important and powerful. I felt the need to repeat it three times—not to bore you, but rather to drill it into your head. If your religions take offense with anything in this book, it will likely be this law.

Questions:
- Are you beginning to understand how far-reaching infinity is?
- And how poorly we understand it?

Actions:
> As important as it is for you to see these truths, it's just as important to recognize society's lies. They have always

been the staples of your beliefs. That's why I've been harping on them. Now I'm asking you to take them and write about how badly they have always fucked up your life.

- ➤ Where the lies are concerned, it's okay to feel the burn, but let it pass on through. Live it.
- ➤ But these truths take it all from your head and put it in your heart—experience it, live it, and cherish it with humble respect.

>>><<<

#32—*There is no good or bad, right or wrong. It is all God.*

There are things only we can conceive of as having a *from* and a *to*—a duality—things that are NOT about the PHYSICAL world. Those are about us and our judgmental minds. The mind of God has no beginning or end. In this world, there is the energy of our thoughts, and ONLY in the energy of our judgmental thoughts does there exist the energy of what is not love, but fear. God has no fear.

Good and bad, right and wrong, evil and . . . Yeah, all that judgmental shit is regurgitated from what is between our ears. We have no problem opening up our mouths and showing that shit off.

Were we to consider ourselves as being on the stage of life, giving EVERYONE a show, would we ever consider dropping our drawers and taking a dump in public?

And yet, we think nothing of opening our mouths and letting all that judgmental shit ooze out.

It is OUR OWN shit. It doesn't exist out here in the physical world—until you spit it out. Even then, it is not exactly the same as in anyone else's mind.

Questions:
- Do you see how simple this law is?
- Are you becoming aware of the depth of its meaning?

Actions:
- ➤ This law epitomizes the heart of society's lies. Elaborate on it.
- ➤ The lies of society here are pretty obvious, aren't they?
- ➤ There is more on this one, and you likely won't see it coming.
- ➤ Watch for it.

#33—*Everything that happens in your life happens for your highest good.*

Your soul orchestrates your life. You are your soul AND an actual part of God, remember? Would God want anything less than the highest and best for *you*?

Another way of stating this law is: *Life is always perfect just as it is—right here, right now.*

Questions:
- Damn! Did I just repeat myself—AGAIN? Laws #20, #30, #31.
- Can you see how it *is* a repeat? Just with a different scenario?
- Are you seeing how these laws—these truths—are as the tapestry of life?
- How it is all woven together?

Actions:
- ➤ What would be a lie that society tells about this law? Elaborate with more than one. There are many.
- ➤ Clue: Every lie can be summated, first by our judgments and then by blame. Blame is always a lie. Which law makes it so? Write.

#34—*The heart wants what the heart wants. As it is your soul directing your heart, the soul seeks what the soul needs.*

The heart is something you physically feel—not so with your soul.

You are disconnected from your soul by this consciousness. Your soul's energy is your highest part. It is connected consciously with the energy of that Highest Power—God.

But like you, it doesn't know a thing until it has experienced it. You are the bridge connecting it all to this world. Your soul, too, needs the experience to "know," as does God.

Questions:
- Are you getting a clue as to why creating life is so important to God?
- Do you see how your life is about your soul's needs?
- But beyond that, what is the service to God?
- Yes, it is confusing being that it is about different aspects of ourselves, right?
- Much easier to just talk as if it were about three separate entities, isn't it?

Actions:
- ➤ What would be a lie that society tells about this law? Elaborate with more than one.
- ➤ Do you think that the leaders of our religions don't know this?
- ➤ Or is it that they don't see us as capable of knowing?
- ➤ Or does it serve to keep us controlled by confusion?
- ➤ Write down what you think—and it is okay if you don't agree.

#35—*We have absolute abundance, limited only by our belief in ourselves—in who we are—as God.*

If our needs—physical, mental, or spiritual—are lacking, it is really our belief that is lacking. Abundance is the yardstick of our belief in our connection to the source, to our belief in God, to the oneness of us all.

Seeing the unlimited abundance in life, you no longer need to seek security in yours.

Questions:
- Is there somewhere in your life that you are lacking?
- Is there something in your life that you want and don't have?
- You do know that YOU actually are the Creator of it, limited only by your belief in that as fact, right?
- Is it possible there is a belief you may have that keeps you from being or having that thing? Something you have—or are—that serves you somehow, but prevents it?

Actions:
- Make a list of what you want but don't now have.
- Why? Everything begins as a thought, so it is ALWAYS your thinking preventing you.
- If it is a relationship with a particular person, remember the laws. You don't get to run anyone else's life but your own.
- Make a list of all the attributes about him or her that you find so attractive. Get clear on who that is.
- Whatever those attributes are, don't go searching for them "out there" but become them—honestly—"in here."
- You will find that person will appear in your life. You just need to recognize him or her.
- Most of all, if you are seeking love, be love.

#36—*We can't give what we don't have in abundance inside.*

To give away what we need for our own sustenance is to commit spiritual suicide—a martyr's knife to the heart of your soul. Worse than the simple lie of blame, it is an attempt to absolve yourself from responsibility for your failure in creating abundance. You are the Creator. As such, it is only your lack of belief in that—as fact—that keeps you from absolute abundance.

Questions:
- Ah, yes, one of society's worst lies is that you have to give to others until you, in your own life, are suffering— even unto death. D'ya know that one?
- Doesn't work there any more than it does when you want someone's love. If that is so, it can only be that you have no love to give them to start with. Do you love yourself? (That's another thing society lies about—that you're a terrible person to love yourself.)
- Do you know that one, too?

Action:
- ➢ There are many lies that society tells about all this. When you finish this section on Spiritual Laws, think about it. You will soon come to realize just how badly society has lied. Then come back and elaborate.

>>><<<

#37—*Living is a conscious choice. Dying is also a choice—usually an unconscious one.*

We live our lives until we have either completed our purpose or quit. Truly living requires courage. As for our purpose, we are an actual part and piece of God. Our purpose is often so grandiose, as to be scary. Few people live so honestly as to consciously conceive it. Of those who do, most don't have the courage to aspire to it, so they quit. Those who don't quit—yeah, they are the SUPERSTARS of life!

Questions:
- There are all kinds of living. Do you see that "how" you choose to live is a conscious thing?
- Just as you, right now, are making a conscious choice to play on the field of life or sit in the bleachers, reading. What is your choice?

Actions:
- ➤ If you are not playing in the game of life, then likely, you have skipped reading this part. Choose better.
- ➤ Knowing what I've been telling you about society, what do you guess society's advice would be here? Write.
- ➤ Assuming you want to be a Superstar, start by making a list of what you are passionate about and what, in your life, gives you joy. Go from there.

>>><<<

#38—*Our world is one of duality. Without duality, we could not know love—or come to know God.*

Love is the bridge connecting us and God. It spans the abyss of all that is not love. It takes this experience here, of knowing what love is not, for our souls to know what love is. God is love—infinite love.

In our world of duality, there is black and white, hot and cold, sweet and sour, night and day . . . always a beginning and an end. Even our thinking runs in duality. There are things we think are good and things we think are evil. Then there are things we see as right and things we see as wrong, a life of caring to one of not.

As in white to black, there is the process in between—the progressing of grays.

The truth is: *There is only love and everything that it is not* (Law #3). In God's truth, this is the only place that does not have a gray area but only an abyss between.

It takes this world of duality for our souls to know God. All that is not love exists only in our own minds in shades of gray. In God's world of infinity, on this there is NO gray. We—man/womankind—need duality to exist on this plane. God does not. This is why Law #3 is so jarring to our minds.

If we are as God's taste buds tasting this life, we are also that part of God where God tastes fear. Without being this little part of God that often fears, could God ever have that experience? Isn't it our fear that forms that abyss between this world and God? Is this fear the true reason we all die and get to return to God? Does it not make sense in explaining why our trips to this world are so short in their very nature? And why for those here, there is joy in the arrivals and suffering in those leaving?

Questions:
- Hell, consider: Does infinity even exist in this earthly realm of duality?
- Can you think of anything that doesn't have a duality—a beginning and an end? Even a starting degree of feeling to an ending, as in love to hate, etc.?
- How about a life of caring, to one of not caring, abdicating it with "don't give a shit"?
- What about these laws themselves? Isn't there the honesty of the Creator, bearing responsibility for what is created, to the dishonesty of the liar, abdicating all responsibility for it by blaming?

Actions:
- ➢ What would be a lie that society tells about this law? Elaborate with more than one.
- ➢ Do you recall how, in the beginning of this book, I explained why I repeat myself?

> Write about all this—and do it with originality.

>>><<<

#39—*Love is the natural way of being. We are always living in love or crying for love.*

The energy must flow (Law #6). It is the energy of our fear that pushes us to love—to God—if we will but let it flow, let go, and let God.

Questions:
- Y'know, it takes a lot more energy to hold a frown than it does a smile, agreed?
- Why would it not also be true with fear and love?

Actions:
> The next time you find yourself frowning, change it to a smile.
> And yup—write about what change you may then notice about yourself or the world around you.
> What would be a lie that society tells about this law? Or do you think society would even know you made it a conscious choice?

>>>END OF LAWS COVERED IN BOOK THREE<<<

#40—*Love is not "doing." It is "being."*

Love is not something you do. Love is a state of "being." You cannot truly love anyone until love is who you choose to be.

Questions:
- Did you find this one confusing?
- Do you see that it really is a choice?
- Do you understand why there is no big-ass explanation?
- Can there be for a no-brainer like this?

Actions:
> ➢ The next time you find yourself trying to love someone or something that is not loveable—stop. Let it be. Your judgments will fade away.
> ➢ Try just accepting that as the way it, or they, are.

#41—*Love makes all life functional.*

It is only in the energy of love that one can find peace. Yeah, this is another no-brainer.

Questions:
- Can you think of anything that falls within the energy of fear that leaves you accepting that person and/or being at peace with them?
- Would you just naturally try to change them somehow?
- Maybe you would instead try to "make them pay"?
- Y'know, you don't have to like someone to accept them. They have a right to be any kind of asshole they want. And maybe that would be the loving thing to do, assuming they are not harming anyone in any physical way.
- Would your own world fall apart if you accepted it as their right to be an asshole?
- Could you actually do that and not try to change them? Do you think you might even get to a place where you no longer see them as such?

Action:
> ➢ Give it a shot, then write about what changes in your life.

#42—*It is only in the chaotic energy of fear where there is dysfunction.*

If your life is dysfunctional, you have only to acknowledge your fears and have the courage to move beyond them.

"Acknowledge your fears?" HOLY CRAP! It's so much easier just to blame it all on someone, or something, else.

Questions:
- Do you see how this last law was about taking chaos and making it functional through love?
- Do you see that this is just a repeat of that law, only now looking at it from the other end?
- Do you see how it ALL depends on YOU changing YOU?
- How YOU don't have the option, or the ability, to change THEM?

Action:
- ➢ Change of viewpoint once again. How is it that you, choosing love, changes your own life much more so than anyone else's? Elaborate on that one.

>>><<<

#43—*Both the control of others and owning of things are myths—lies we are convinced are truth.*

Just as we cannot respect anyone we can control, owning a thing we have not paid a price for gives it NO value in our minds. The value we place on a thing, or the respect that we have for a person—THAT is ALL we own.

As stated in Law #5: "*. . .for every joyful thing one gets, there is a price to be paid.*" Again, the Universe always balances. There are no free lunches.

When we pay for something in the script of our energy. That energy becomes something we actually do own—forever. Our energy is all we will ever own.

Questions:
- Do you want that energy to ever be other than loving?
- Do you understand that value and respect are both judgments that exist only in our own mind?

- What you place value on, or have respect for, will, in the mind of someone else, never be exactly the same?
- You may own a dog, and you may feel love for another person. Again, that love that YOU, yourself, feel is all you truly own. Do you understand the distinction?
- Whether it is the love they give you or the control they allow, there is nothing there for you to own?
- And things? Things don't have feelings. Ownership . . . allegiance? Things don't have a mind to give a shit about you. You are their custodian in your own mind, at best.

Actions:

- ➢ Has anything here touched you? Do you see it differently now? Write.
- ➢ Society does not see it this way, do they? Elaborate.

#44—*Like love, respect must start with respecting ourselves. It, too, is a state of being.*

If we are lacking in the being, how can we be anything other than stingy in the giving? Surround yourself with those you love. Respect them. Then reach out to those others. Find something about them you can love or, at least, just appreciate. Respect them for having that quality. The love and respect you give to others is reflected back to become a part of you.

Questions:

- With others, isn't love and respect a gift you think you are giving them? In reality, it is a gift you give to yourself in your feelings toward them, isn't it?
- They cannot physically feel your feelings, can they?
- Is it not just incorporated within your choice of feeling love?
- Can you see it as something that never comes about within the space of any fear?

Actions:
- ➤ Any love you give to others is your feelings that only you actually get to feel. Write about that.
- ➤ Now I ask you, have I slapped you upside the head enough with this concept here? Your choice in loving others is something only you own. Above all, it is your gift to you. It is something others recognize and can appreciate as being *you*. Yup—write about it, and about the lie that society tells about it.

>>><<<

#45—*Emotions are the words of the soul and are fueled by its unmet needs.*

If it's in your face, it's a lesson, a message, or a test validating and acknowledging your learning. It is up to you to correctly interpret the emotion.

This explanation was since taught to me by Dale Holloway, a mentor, friend, and kindred spirit. I have never heard it from any other source.

Questions:
- • Your emotions are your soul's way of saying, "Look at this. Ask yourself why you feel this way." Do you see that it is your soul's way of pointing out something you need to see about you?
- • If the feeling feels good, it is saying, "Gimme more." Yes?
- • If bad, it says, "Change something about the way you perceive this." Uh-huh?

Actions:
- ➤ Do you always follow the promptings of your soul?
- ➤ What happens when you don't?
- ➤ Did Dale Holloway's message help you understand?
- ➤ Is society's demand that you blame others for your feelings a functional thing to do? **Elaborate on it all.**

>>><<<

#46—*The meeting of needs is the glue that holds a relationship together.*

Needs are the driving force behind every relationship. Love cannot suffice without meeting one another's fearful needs. The non-fearful needs—the need to give and receive love—are the icing on the cake. The fearful needs are the lessons needed to get us to love. It could be said that relationships are the schoolground for the lessons of love.

The real essence of this law is simply that in relationships, you both are giving the other the opportunity to grow beyond those fearful needs.

For some, their relationships have nothing to do with love, but most would likely agree that relationships are supposed to be about love.

Yet no matter what the needs may be, for relationships to work, the meeting of needs must exist for both. For when one's needs are not being met, they become the driving force in one's life—the force that drives the relationship apart.

In the duality of this world, LOVE is the energy that all who hold other energies (FEAR) aspire to have.

In short, this describes why we are all here to learn our lessons—indeed, what our lessons are about. When we fail to get the lessons that our significant other is in our life to give us, THAT is what drives us apart. It necessitates the need to find someone else we will accept the lessons from.

Questions:
- Beyond the giving and receiving of love, can you think of even one need that isn't based on fear?
- Can you think of even one need that, once met, hasn't resulted in love?

- Are you in a relationship now, and if so, is there a lot of drama?
- Are you aware that drama is ALWAYS about someone's need for control (fear)?

Actions:

- ➢ If you answered "yes" to the last two questions, write about it.
- ➢ How much of your relationships are based on control dramas and fear? Again, write.
- ➢ This is the biggie concerning all our lives—in fact, in understanding our whole world.
- ➢ This is the SECRET behind Law #3, the secret of why you exist here in this world. Get it? **Write about it.**

#47—*Every action has its reaction.*

Living life is like playing a game of billiards. You don't always know who will be impacted by your actions. It's up to you to make your actions loving. Then those impacted will be touched by your love. The energy transferred will always be loving. And you must be aware that it will not always be perceived as loving.

There is always action and reaction—*cause and effect*. And then there are *consequences*. Those are about others judging you wrong and getting revenge. Judgments are built by perceptions, and perception often has little to do with "what is"—what is the truth.

Questions:

- How has your energy been impacting those around you?
- Loving?
- Or not loving?
- Do you see that "consequences" always spring from man's judgmental mind?

Actions:
- ➢ This one, too, is as big as the law just before it. Think about it.
- ➢ In all that you say and do in life, make your energy be loving.
- ➢ Reactions are what happen before there is judgment. Make certain that your reactions are never about judgment and revenge.
- ➢ Understand that this will not stop society's lies. Likely, you will still be blamed for other people's shit. They will not like you for making it hard to do, but you will know who you want to hold close to in your life. Write about it.

#48—*Perception is a choice.*

This is the area where everything gets sticky. The big choice here is, do you live and think in the energy of love—or fear. *You* are the *Creator* of your life. If you live your life in love, these laws will be perceived with love. But when living in fear, they may have other meanings entirely.

If you've gotten this far with these laws, and IF what is rolling through the creative pathways of your mind are words of fear—words like *bullshit, lies, fucked up*—well then, guess what energy you are living in and creating your life by? The positive, loving side of it lies in the fact that you are reading this. That says it all. IT IS YOUR CRY FOR LOVE. There is no other possible reason.

And it is your choice, your decision, in the creation of yourself. If words of fear are slithering through your mind right now, you can change them, but it will take a huge inner rejection of much about yourself—a rejection that can only come from hitting the bottom of that cesspool you have created surrounding yourself.

You will need to want love with a passion unlike anything you have ever experienced. *That* is what it will take.

Too simple? Or too difficult? Take heart, as it is also the pathway of a hero—someone who has grown far beyond what most everyone else has had the opportunity to become. Life is not always about who you are, but rather, who you have become. And more, who you will become. *Life is a journey, and for you—now—a hero's journey.*

Question:
  • Where did the term "hero's journey" originate?

Actions:
  ➢ You don't have to agree, but if you want to be your own hero, you DO have to step through the fear stopping you. Courage is what heroes are all about.
  ➢ Society doesn't want you taking this journey. If you are solidly on this path, you will see it. Elaborate.

>>><<<

#49—*All emotional pain is self-created, and all physical pain carries a necessary ingredient of self-creation.*

This is simply another direct aspect of *Law #1: I am the Creator.* It is mentioned separately here only because it is the part where most people get most heavily into blame. It is simply very difficult not to recognize how chickenshit blame really is when one won't take responsibility for what they clearly create in their own head—their thinking—and their resulting feelings. We do it because it is what our society has taught us to do.

Society is about controlling other people. Who is more easily controlled than someone who sees themselves as a victim? You can then victimize them with impunity. Every person and every group wants to control you. They are your "society."

Religions are just such a group on steroids. Most Christian religions teach that God, or Jesus, will save you from your feelings—hell, save you from your whole life. God or Jesus will do it all for you, *they say*. Without your ability to respond (your responsibility), you become a victim in life—a controllable victim. Again, it is about control.

Do you see how all of the Spiritual Laws revolve around your "responsibilities"—where your ability to respond *is* in life?

Questions:
- Can you see how it is so much easier to blame others and circumstances?
- Do you see how you make yourself a victim through blame?
- How about this: You give away all your power to control your life when you don't take responsibility?
- Do you realize that responsibility is a full-time thing?

Actions:
- ➢ Only one action is required: *You never get to blame anyone or anything for your feelings ever again.*
- ➢ Write about why this is so.

>>><<<

#50—What is of true evil in this life is created in your mind through the process of determining "what is good and what is bad"—and especially in "what is right and wrong."

Those things do not exist outside one's own mind. And inside, they are only lies—lies your judgmental mind conjures up to make your own life work for you. It is evil for you to demand that it be so for me.

We are talking about CONTROL—also spelled as P-O-W-E-R.

Whether held in the hands of the preacher at church or your government leaders, POWER CORRUPTS. It resides at the end of the duality of mankind—the power end of his heart away from the love.

Give him a sword of power, and he will cut his heart away from love every time with evil. Given the power to make anything "right" in his corrupt mind, no amount of evil is beyond him.

No matter how you judge something, it has to be right in your own mind. When it is not so in mine is when evil is created by you in my life.

Questions:
- Everything Hitler ever did you can be sure was "right" in his own mind. If it wasn't, then he would have had a real problem living with himself. Knowing this, is it hard to see how evil is something that can only exist in the mind of man?
- And too, do you see why he had a need for everyone else in the Third Reich to see it his way?

Actions:
- ➤ Be aware that the potential for evil exists in your own mind.
- ➤ If you want someone to be other than they are badly enough, you, too, WILL create evil. Where did you create evil? Write about it.
- ➤ And having done so, you, too, will seek validation. In fact, you will demand it from those around you. For most, it just brands you as an asshole. For others who wield power in government, some may get sent to prison over it. Write about that.
- ➤ But when there is a person of power or importance involved, they might just get away with anything—Hitler did. Know anyone like that in today's world? Write about it.

#51—*This life—this part of God's experience—is your true destiny.*

As with all living beings, we are *the* part of God that gets to experience life and, in so doing, gets to *know* life!

On this conscious level, you think you are learning these things, and having learned, know. Thing is, you cannot truly *"know"* without experiencing. This is the part where you contribute to the whole of God's experience of life. Again, as with all living things, we are *as the taste buds of God tasting—life!*

It is also where your soul gets its critical need to "know" by experiencing it in your own life. Again, that eighteen-inch journey from the head to the heart—THAT is what life is all about. Your destiny is the taking of that journey with your soul, and essentially, with God also.

Questions:
- Again, adding experience is clearly the catalyst for "knowing" life, don't you think?
- Adding appreciation to the lessons in a failed relationship is also a catalyst, isn't it?
- Can you see that both your life and your relationships cannot be complete without the catalyst of experience?
- **Can you also see how with both**, neither is a failure once that catalyst of appreciation is "known"?
- On the relationship side, that catalyst is obviously a thing of love.

Actions:
- ➢ Could it ever be otherwise when experiencing life in the energy of love? Make it always so in your own life.
- ➢ And write about that.

#52—*You always have exactly what you want in life.*

You are the Creator of your life, constantly creating—all of it. If it's in your life, you created it being there.

You cannot change anything you don't like about your life unless you can see why you created it. How does it serve you? It does serve you, y'know?

If it didn't, it would no longer be there. If your aggravation were enough to expel it, it would be gone. It is always better to replace it with something that serves you better without any aggravation. Or maybe just to look at your judgmental beliefs and change the ones that give rise to your feelings.

Questions:
- Is there anything in your life that you don't want?
- How does it serve you? You can't change it unless you can see this.

Actions:
- ➢ Make a list of everything in your life that you DON'T like.
- ➢ Now list how those things serve you.
- ➢ If you don't know, it can only be because you don't want to know, usually because if you did, your whole life would need to change.
- ➢ Figuring this out could be the highest and best this book has to offer you. Set the question to your soul with honest intent, knowing it will take courage. There will be a price you will pay in knowing. Then relax and accept the answer. Your soul will give it to you in its perfect time.

>>><<<

#53—*How every religion perceives the afterlife—heaven—to be is always the truth.*

Don't make light of anyone's spiritual beliefs. They are all true. If you can conceive of how you absolutely create your reality here on Earth, why wouldn't you know that, on the other side, you will be not only an absolute but an instant Creator? Wouldn't heaven be exactly as you perceive it and create it?

There certainly are those three degrees of glory in the judgmental Mormon heaven, just as there is a Catholic heaven and an equally vindictive Catholic hell. Every heaven is a creation of ours—of mankind.

No matter how sanctimonious your creation, your heaven is exactly as you believe it to be. And God, the Great Omnipotent Deity of it all—the everywhere, within everything God—gives you the infinite dimensions of space and time to make it so.

Questions:
- Did this law blow your mind?
- Given the meaning and truth in all these Spiritual Laws, how could it be otherwise?
- Do you really think God, that Higher Power, gives a rat's ass if you are good or evil? Or how you conceive of Him/Her/It—or heaven?

Actions:
- ➤ YOU provide God's experiences of sentient life. Does that not require ALL of it—the full gamut—for God to know this life? Kinda goes against the grain with most Christian religions, true? So, write about what you think.
- ➤ Perhaps that is because the concept of God and heaven, even hell, is a fabrication of man. It is also required for God to experience and to know of this—His creation called mankind.

➤ Perhaps with all of God's vast experiencing of the love of man, God just might prefer the experiencing of the unconditional love of mankind's pet dog. Write about that.

>>><<<

#54—*In creating everything in life, love conquers all.*

Everything you create in life begins with your energy. And everyone you touch and influence is also influenced by that energy.

Most will tell you that the process of creation begins with your thoughts, then your words, then your deeds. No. The defining factor of what you create is your energy. We are all beings of energy, and we do affect others just by our presence. Make yours loving.

If you are faced by a group—or even just one person—whose energy is not at all loving, and if your purpose is to bring about calm, if your own energy is that of fear, it will be impossible. Positive change can only be accomplished if your energy is that of love. Love cannot exist in the space of fear, nor can fear exist in the space of love.

Question:

• Perhaps for most, we have been taught to be victims—fear-filled victims. To be anything more requires courage. It takes courage to step past one's fears. Do you have the courage?

Actions:

➤ The good thing about doing that is when one lives in the energy of love, there's no longer need for courage.
➤ The bad thing is, this life is always one of duality, and we need the experience. To exist in that space of love, we need to have lived in fear and had the courage to step through it.
➤ Write about it.

>>><<<

#55—*The only reason you allow someone to be in your personal life is because they serve yours in some way.*

The only thing you must determine is, do they serve in a functional manner? And do you serve them likewise?

Question:
- Our life, and those who are in it, are on a two-way street. Is there someone haunting your life and you don't know why?

Actions:
- List everyone who is in your life and, whether you like or don't like them. Now figure out why they stay there—how in being there, they serve you.
- Maybe you would do well to consider why you are in their life. What gift do you bear them in theirs? Often, the gift for you is found in the giving.

>>><<<

>>>END OF LAWS COVERED IN BOOK FOUR<<<

#56—*Sex is not love. It is an action that may be performed in the energy of love. It is a need. One that everyone has a need to do.*

What is sex? It's basically the process by which we procreate—keep this world populated. It would never serve that function were it not enjoyable.

Ah, but our species takes that purpose to extremes. Our perception of it can get real fucked up (no pun intended). We use it to inflict pain or humiliation, to hurt or demean someone else in our own eyes. Or just to make one's dick feel good at the expense of others, as in rape.

Then there is fulfilling our kinky, little fantasies. Holy shit, that one is a bucket of worms. And speaking of shit . . . yeah, some like it in that end, too.

Bottom line is, yes, it could just be an expression of two people in love, wanting to pleasure one another, but sex is NOT love.

Questions:
- Do you refer to sex as "making love?"
- Doesn't that serve to make all the more negative or selfish fucking also into being something called love?

Actions:
- ➢ Find another way to refer to it. Maybe "noodling with the noodle."
- ➢ Or whammy, as in "gimme some whammy."
- ➢ If you're kinky and looking at it backward, how about "plugging the poo."
- ➢ But please, don't demean love by calling sex "making love" unless your intent is to pleasure the person you love, maybe more so than yourself.

>>><<<

#57—*There are no selfless acts. No one does anything whereby it does not benefit one's own self in some way.*

It is wise to know what that benefit is for another's action . . . wiser still to know what it is for your own.

Society has a shitload of lies calling for the opposite—shirt-off-your-back bullshit. If you look closely at those lies, you will most likely see the drama of the martyr showing clearly.

What does that mean to be a martyr? You set yourself up on a pedestal, above everyone else. You get to be BETTER than— more noble than—all others.

There are whole religions wherein people play the martyr by blowing themselves up, killing hundreds of innocents, just to get on that pedestal.

Sick fucking shit!

Even when done on a less grisly scale, it is STILL sick fucking shit!

Question:
- Do you see what it means to "know thyself"?

Action:
- ➢ Keep this law in mind if you intend to be wise.

#58—*One's wants are governed by one's needs. Of course, there are the physical needs of life. Aside from that, ultimately, one's needs are the soul's needs—the spiritual lessons of the soul.*

It is rarely apparent what the connection is to the lesson one's soul is teaching them right now. Just know that their soul is one with yours. And the lessons one's soul teaches are the same for them as they are for you.

If you want to be loved, then the soul's lessons about what love is are critical needs to know. The truth about love is something few people know.

Questions:
- What particular lessons has your soul been teaching you?
- Do you even have a clue?

Actions:
- ➢ Don't stress on discovering the answer. Just hold this thought in the back of your mind. Your soul will give you the answer—or not—depending if you need to know.

➤ Do you intend to be of service by sharing your experience in honest humility with others? That would be a nice touch.

≫≫≪≪

#59—*The perceived value is equal to the conceived cost.*

When something comes at no monetary price, it's hard to see the value. In my Personal Life Coaching practice, those pro bono clients were all into personal growth work—they said. The price they paid for my coaching was for them to step out of their comfort zone. Not all could even fathom that as a cost or see the value, since most equate price and value with money. As for me, my value in coaching them was found in the experience.

Question:
- Did you know that Personal Life Coaching is not about what the coach wants of you?
- It is about discovering what you want and then supporting you in getting it.
- It is about you deciding what steps you are willing to take. The coach only provides someone to whom you need to answer.
- It is about your coach being your own personal cheering section.
- Coaching is about all the above. More than that, it's about doing your own fucking thinking—something most don't understand. Do you?

Action:
➤ As a coach, I discovered the main obstacle my clients faced was the myriad of lies they were taught to run their lives by. The lies ALWAYS resulted in dysfunction. Once they learned the simple truths of life—the Spiritual Laws—they had little use for me. LEARN THE TRUTHS OFFERED IN THESE BOOKS.

>>><<<

#60—*Helping is really taking when it is saving others from doing something they have the ability to do for themselves.*

In the doing, you are robbing them of the experience their soul has tasked them to learn— something they need to learn in order to have the ability to do for themselves. YOU are cheating THEM of learning to be who THEY want to be in life.

Questions:
- Do you agree?
- If not, where else is this concept fucking you over in life?
- Did you take offense with the way I voiced this last question?
- Do you collect a stipend from the government welfare system?
- If so, does it stop you from supporting yourself and rob you of your self-respect?
- With some it is "helping"—for others, "saving." Which is it for you?

Action:
- ➢ Oh . . . write about that.

>>><<<

#61—*I am responsible for my feelings and will hold you capable and responsible for yours.*

Same concept as Law #13 and Law #60, different application.

Question:
- How is this the same concept?

Actions:
- ➢ Write down your own thoughts about it.
- ➢ Don't take my thoughts as Gospel. *Think for yourself.*

>>><<<

#62—*Making someone else responsible for our happiness is never functional, just as taking responsibility for their unhappiness is not also.*

No one can "make" you happy. Nor can you be the responsible party to "making" them happy.

This is the flipside of Law #61. Laws #13, #60, #61 and #62 all have a common denominator. They all center directly on responsibility—the ability to respond.

Questions:
- Who do you think it is who ALWAYS has the ability to respond when feelings are the issue?

Action:
- ➢ Go back over EVERY law given to this point and ask yourself this question: Does it have a common denominator of feelings—whose feelings?

>>><<<

LAW #63—*When we don't accept the truth of "what is," we guarantee ourselves pain.*

Pain is the place where the seagull shits—the birthplace of "blame." Most in this world would do anything rather than be the responsible party to their own pain. Like a seagull they dump their shit on others.

Questions:
- When was the last time you felt emotional pain?
- Who or what did you blame it on?
- Physical pain? Who volunteers for that? Yes, it is almost always created unconsciously.

Actions:

➤ Stop being such a namby-pamby pussy. Place the responsibility where it always lies in your life—with YOU.

➤ Stop walking around under seagulls. You will collect a lot less seagull shit. Kinda hard to wipe that off on other people.

>>><<<

#64—*If it's in your face, it's either a lesson, a message, or a test from your soul, validating and acknowledging your learning.*

This law was previously used in explaining Law #45. It deserves to be its own law and is so listed. It is important to know that those things that gripe your ass are ALWAYS messages from your soul.

Questions:

• Have you had anything happen recently that really got your panties in a bunch?

• Do you think it was a lesson or a message?

• If you got the message or lesson, the tests are then generally about what once would have griped your ass but no longer does. Which is it?

Action:

➤ Write about it.

>>><<<

#65—*To show SYMPATHY for someone is to set yourself up as above—better than—them and serves only to lower the energy of both. Showing EMPATHY is a gift you give that raises you both.*

Unless it is something you have also experienced, you don't have the ability to show honest sympathy. But you always have it to empathize.

Questions:
- Which is loving and which is not?
- Do you know the difference? Society doesn't.

Action:
➤ Get the necessary humility and choose empathy in the future.

#66—*The meeting of needs is the glue that holds a relationship together. Needs are the driving force behind every relationship. Love cannot suffice without meeting one another's fearful needs.*

What most people call love is often just one of those fearful needs. The real essence of this law is simply that in relationships, you both are giving the other the opportunity to grow beyond those fearful needs—something one person cannot do alone.

Questions:
- Have you ever seen a relationship where one person claims the other as "property"—and then calls it love?
- Or sees their jealousy as love?
- Have YOU ever been that person?

Action:
➤ Make a list of other things of fear that are also claimed to be a person's "love."

#67—*It can be more joyous to parent a child who is of your heart than one merely of your flesh.*

Holding on to the child you can't have guarantees you will never be satisfied with the one you can. It also guarantees that child's life will be devastated.

This law is one I learned from personal experience. For me to even see it is only because of knowing these truths, these

Spiritual Laws. I have mentioned it to you who may be considering adopting a child—and more as a gift for that child.

(Curious? You can read the story in my book, *The Courage of a Butterfly*.)

Question:
  • Do you want to adopt **THAT** child, or just **A** child?
Action:
  ➤ Write about what you think this question is REALLY asking.

>>><<<

#68—*Gratitude is our way of thanking that Higher Power. Gratitude raises one's energy beyond the natural evolution of one's soul.*

Nothing your soul learns in life is ever complete without gratitude.

Question:
  • Do you have gratitude?
Actions:
  ➤ Make a list of all the things you recently have cause for thanking the Creator.
  ➤ Do you know *you just did!*

>>><<<

#69—*The energy of fear is always a cry for love.*

Remember there are only the two energies: There is the energy of love, and there is the energy of everything that is not love (fear).

The love you give to others comes from an abundance of love energy you have within you. But what if you don't have much love, even for yourself? What then, is the extent of the energy you have to give to others?

Is the "love" you have to give really only fear energy. Are you someone who is crying for love.

Questions:
- How can fear energy be anything other than a cry for love?
- Can you see why that fear energy, in any of its various forms, can ONLY be a cry for love?
- But there is that other law: ***The energy out, returns in kind***.
- It takes someone with a great abundance of love to go against that law. Can you see that?

Actions:
- ➢ This law was mentioned previously in support of Law #48. Go back and reread it.
- ➢ Be someone who lives their own life in the energy of love until such time when YOU are that abundant. Until then, refrain from being that person who returns the fear.

PART THREE
Spirituality

Spirituality—it's not something you occasionally feel. It is what you are in every moment of time. You see it—you feel it—you live it—from what you eat to what you excrete, it nurtures you. You are clothed in the very fabric of Spirituality. It is the experience of life.

NOTE:
What follows here is a series of pictures of life illuminated by the Spiritual Laws. Unlike the first four books in this series, which pointed out specifically which laws were involved with that particular picture, this book leaves that up to you to discover. In your workbooks, with each picture, YOU fill in a section titled "Laws" for each picture. Many times, there will be more than one law involved.

About This Redneck Spirituality Series

I wrote this *Redneck Spirituality* series about New Thought and Spiritual Law in an effort to give you a picture of what the truth is about life. After four books, I considered hanging up my writing—figured I'd pretty much said all I had to say.

Meanwhile, so much has happened: Covid 19 and the shutting down of life as we knew it—our freedoms all taken away under that pretext. The rise of Antifa and their destructive riots burning down our civilization—race division as in Black Lives Matter (BLM). The theft of an election and the resulting bumbling administration's intentional erasing of everything our nation has ever stood for in this world—yes, INSANITY!

Where do I start? Maybe with our government with its left and right. It's always been there, but now it's as a battlefield with real dead bodies. And woke? They're like the Taliban of the left. As a writer, it's overwhelming. Is mankind like a humongous boil on the ass end of this world, festering, just waiting for it all to come to a head and explode?

Me? I wonder if all this Liberal shit is the Shariah law end of normal thinking. And thinking? I believe there are only two basic ways of looking at life: Either you run your own life, or, as we have all been taught from birth, you see other people as running your life and blame them when it is fucked up. Yes, we have all been taught to see life as victims with others in control.

Say, what? VICTIMS? It's only natural to believe those in authority, but victims? How do you figure?

Yeah, I can hear y'all now, but think about it. In those first years of life, our parents told us what to do, when to do it, and how to see this world. Yes, and we believed them. Never mind that their main focus was on controlling us, making us behave the way they wanted—at least in the beginning. It is only later that they started teaching us lies about how the world works. And you can't blame them. You are their progeny. They expect you to carry on their lives after they're gone from this world.

And so, they taught you everything the same way they learned it. For most, their own inheritance was that of their parents' perceptions, just as yours now is for you.

It is the way this world basically thinks. Most everyone in it is focused on getting other people to live in a way that suits themself. Trying to control those around you is just what victims feel the need to do.

Everyone wants to see themselves as the master, but in reality, they believe themselves a victim. For our society, is fighting and controlling others really the easier way, the better way? Better than just accepting others as being different? Wanting everyone to be the same as you is what most see as being at peace. The reality of such a world is boredom.

Now, we are talking about our society. You see, becoming a victim of whoever is doing the controlling takes a shitload of lies because the truth is, *we run our own lives*. But whether we are running it our own way or someone else's, we nonetheless run it ourselves. Therein lies the struggle.

And the simple truth of life? It is all a matter of perspective— the actuality of how we see our life, or the actuality of how we want to see it. Never mind the actuality of what the truth is about life. Yeah, I'm talking about the Spiritual Laws.

Think about it. Doesn't our society teach us that in order to be acceptable, we have to show up as being who other people want us to be? We must wear the façade. If we are just being who we are, others won't accept us. That's one of the worst of society's shitload of lies. It serves as the black background to the Spiritual Laws—the big kahuna of which is illuminated by the light of truth.

You are the Creator—especially of your life.

Society's lying rule is guaranteed to fuck with your mind. And yet, every "normal" person believes it. Living in a society where everyone is trying to control everyone else while pretending to be someone who they, themselves, are not . . . how can that be functional? But that is the norm for society.

Yet in the chaos of these times right now, society has been fractured. I, for one, question if there even IS a normal society. The "from and to"—the gamut of it—is now at such extremes. Again, INSANITY!

Where can one turn for sanity? How about to the Spiritual Laws? They're really just the simple truths of life. *They are the natural way of being—the functional way.* What would your life be like if you showed up as being exactly who *you* want to be?

It's true, some people won't like or accept you. But those who do, will, because you are who they would want to be—if they believed they could.

They will then become your friends, real friends. When with you, they feel free to be who they, too, are. That is so liberating. And society? They become your society.

Would you then be just another splinter off the fractured vase of society as a whole? Or could you become the catalyst to building a new vase?

Those in "normal" society will continue living their lies, thinking they are liked and accepted. But are they? When they aren't living true to who they are, how can they be?

No one in the whole busted-up vase of normal society is being real. No one knows who anyone really is. Does that sound functional to you? Seeing you, will they then continue to live the lies of society? Maybe, but maybe not.

All my life, I, too, lived those lies until there came a time when I thought it was over for me. After a lifetime of pretense, I discovered that I didn't know who I was. But I knew I didn't like or respect that person. Regardless of which fucked-up splinter of society you belong to, such a time will come for everyone—including you.

What does any of this have to do with the woke culture that is trying to run this world? Woke is just the far end, you might say the ASS END, of all societies on the left.

And society? Again, we have all been taught to be a victim in life. Only the New Thought folks who follow the Spiritual Laws have stepped out of the quagmire.

But WOKE? That is the maximum for victim-thinking folks. They demand that others step around the eggshells of their itty-bitty fweelings and then take *huge* offense with anyone who doesn't. Can you see that by taking offense, they make themselves a victim? It validates who they see themselves as being.

Taking offense is nothing but a control drama—holding their feelings as ransom to the guilt of your own. Kind of a shitty dysfunction, wouldn't you say? That is why I call them the ass end of normal society.

Offense may, or may not, be intended. Thing is, it cannot be given. It must be taken. When taken, it is like dropping your drawers and taking a dump in the middle of the sidewalk.

You may see it as keeping others from stepping on your fweelings. Truth is, people don't walk around it out of like or respect for you. Y'know?

So those who are "not normal"? Those generally are called New Thought, even though there's nothing new about it. They're simply those folks who base their thinking on the Spiritual Laws—the simple truths of life.

Truth is always the truth, unlike lies, which vary, depending on who it is demanding that you live by them. Everyone knows truth. It's an automatic soul thing. Maybe that is why they are most often called Spiritual Laws.

Thing is, once you become aware of the truth, you then start seeing those lies you spent your life believing—lies you based your life upon.

When consciously seeing them, you change from victim to victor. Once you get a grip on the truth, you won't want to let go.

Again, you are the Creator.

Those lies becomes the elephant dump on your living room floor, something you can never again ignore. You begin to see how previously, in your unconscious ignorance, you have been walking through it, tracking that shit throughout your whole house, and you will begin cleaning it up.

Your house, your life, becomes your own. YOU created it. YOU own it all. It becomes YOUR responsibility. You no longer have the chickenshit luxury of blaming any of it on others.

That law—*You are the Creator*—forms the tapestry of your life. Every thread in the fabric of it is but different aspects of this truth. All the other laws I've been telling you about are simply the "how" of this law.

This book began as a series of "rants" on Facebook. But rants are about the negative shit. It is so much nicer to be slapped upside your face with a book about the truth. The truth doesn't stink. But everything in this life comes in duality, the "from" and the "to." This book comes from the stink of shittery to a breath of ecstasy—the lies of society to the truth.

This is elemental to the truths of life. It has been covered, in fact, has likely reupholstered your life, in the first four books. So, I am only asking these questions of those who haven't read the other books.

Questions:
- Can you see how you have been taught to be a victim?
- Are you still one?

Action:
- ➤ Take responsibility for your life and everything in it.

The Stink of Shit

Again, your beliefs—namely, the ones that were lies that you previously counted on as being the truth. Those are what *don't* work. They have only fucked up your life.

Chances are that someone, some authority figure you probably liked, told them to you to begin with. You took their beliefs, made them your own, and likely never thought another thing about it, same as they once did. That is the "normal" way of learning for "normal" people—always has been.

Like you, that is what's been fucking up most everyone's life since time began. Why? Likely, the why is because they, too, were never told about life's truths. But in reading these books, you will know them. You are—or will be—one of the few who can see those lies. Just know that telling those lies to you was not purposeful. They could not know.

Changing your life has nothing to do with willpower and everything to do with seeing something differently. It's about changing your beliefs.

Again, in life there are truths out there, and there are lies—always have been. But most all of us are taught those lies from childhood and rarely seek out the truth. If you believed what you believe, why would you?

Here is just one of those truths. There are many that are much more important, but this one is key to changing your life.

> *If you change anything about your thinking, you change your whole life. Everything begins as a thought.*

So, okay, you've heard this before. The point being, if you know the truths, you will see the lies and reject believing them. Automatically. Effortlessly. This is the good part, like the sweet smell of a flower.

The Universe always balances. In this world of duality, everything has a from and a to. So, if flowery sweetness is the from, what would be the to? Try this—*the stink of shit!*

What makes the changing effortless is simply that you are sure to reject the shit, flush it clean out of your life. Again, when you know the truth about life, you see the lies, the shit. YOUR shit.

You can't avoid it, nor can you stop yourself from flushing the stink of it. It's one of those personal things that deserves to be done alone in your toilet. No one can do it except you.

Questions:
- Do you see that being "normal" is not necessarily a good thing?

- Do you want to know the truth?

Action:

➢ Keep on reading.

>>><<<

Digging It Deeper

We humans have always done life ass-backward. *Everything we know, everything* we believe has been taught to us by others. And, too, the way we should feel about *everything* was learned from someone else, some authority figure in our younger life. Face it. We have been taught NOT to think for ourselves. I believe that is called by a number of names— brainwashing, mind control, or just mental enslavement.

It is all about lies.

Lies meant to serve others, either in their actual life, their ego, or just to validate their own beliefs. The word for it all is *control*. It is a society thing. "If you don't pretend to be who we want you to be, you won't be accepted by us. We must control you." And so, you wear a variety of façades to the point where you lose track of the truth of who YOU are.

And the truth?

Truth is, we come into this world with only two things from that Higher Power—LIFE and a little TIME to live it. *Now, add to that a third, more important, thing: the right to determine it, to create it all for yourself.*

You—we—are all
The creators of our own life.

Remember that is a God-given right? This third right is accompanied by the ability to use the underlying power of the Universe in making our world work just for us. *Again, our world doesn't exist out there, but rather, in our mind, the way we perceive and believe it to be.*

And the power?

All the power of the Universe "out there" will attract it to you exactly as you perceive it to be "in here." Those three things—rights—are given to you from the Maker. But NOT as a gift, for they carry an expectation for you to

think for yourself.

But those rights have been stolen by the authority figures in our society. Thing is, WE are the ones who give them their authority.

Take it back!

If you can conceive of what I am saying, you must then realize the importance for you to FUCKING think for yourself. The truth of it all is expressed by the Spiritual Laws—the simple truths of life.

THESE TRUTHS ARE YOUR GUIDE.

Questions:
- Do you think that, so far, this book has been shitting in the face of everything you believed about life?
- Are you beginning to see the lies?

Action:
- ➢ Keep on truckin'!

Some Thoughts Deserve a Repeat

Your world is not "out there"—it is "in here." It is composed of every thought, every feeling, every perception you have about EVERYTHING. Therein lies humanity's great downfall.

You see, most all of our thoughts and beliefs are borrowed from what is between someone else's ears. That FACT is what has always put a pall of stench over life on this planet. I call it the "shit for brains syndrome." Taking other people's beliefs and making them your own ALWAYS puts the skids on thinking for yourself. But then again, that doesn't work well, either. Unless you can see the simple truths of life, how can you ever see the lies?

Lies? What the fuck does that mean?

It's reeee-uul simple. Those other people are usually the folks we look up to and hold in some esteem—your parents, your teachers, your religious leaders—in fact, all leaders of our society in general.

The thing no one seems to see is that those people ALL have one goal in mind. Again, that goal is to get you to live your life so that it serves theirs. That might mean anything from simple validation for themselves, to servitude, to outright slavery. It is all about controlling you to suit them. To be fair, they, too, were taught to be victims in life, to have a victim mentality.

As a child, your parents just needed you to behave . . . and to grow up so that your life would follow their own.

Your teachers mindlessly followed the curriculum they were given. The same shit they, too, were taught in their own youth.

Your religions? They teach that everything good you get in life is dispensed by Jesus or God. The devil makes you do all the bad shit. And if you're not happy, blame that on your significant other.

Add to that the fact that society, in general, teaches that in order to be acceptable, you need to wear a façade—a pretense of being who other people would want, that you will never be accepted being who you really are.

But you? Being a victim to everyone and everything around you, you never get to run your own life. And victims? All victims have a *huge* need to control everyone around them.

Yes, this is the "normal" operating procedure for our society. It is a FACT, and is repeated in all of my books.

Questions:
- Do you accept the truth of it?
- Are you understanding the significance of it?

Actions:
- Make a choice to either see yourself as a victim, incapable of running your own life, or to follow this incredibly simple truth—*I am the Creator of my life and everything in it!*
- Choose to not be a victim by accepting this last phrase.

Normal People

We've talked ad nauseam about how we have all been taught to be victims in life. That is very true. It's called "being normal." And the response of "normal" people is blame. If other people, and/or the events of life, are the reason your life sucks, then you don't have to bear ANY responsibility.

Therein lies the kicker. It is really about who is responsible—where the responsibility lies. To understand it requires you to know what the word "responsible" really means.

Try this: It is simply a matter of who has the ability to respond. That leads to the first pivotal, the *holy shit*, of the Spiritual Laws—YOU do.

Spiritual Law #1: I am the Creator. There is NOTHING in my life that I do not have a deciding part in creating!

I AM THE CREATOR OF MY LIFE.

It's true, and cannot be repeated often enough. Oh, but there is much more to it.

When I was a teenager, our family spent a couple of years living in Greece. My father was a boss on a construction project building a diversion tunnel for a dam on the Acheloos River.

It was in the boonies—the Ozarks of Greece—and, as usual, we kids had free rein in roaming the countryside. It was where two rivers joined the Achelous. The deepest one went through a gorge. The water there flowed very slowly. It was so deep that very little movement was apparent on the surface.

Although very clear, one couldn't see the bottom. Even when diving down, it simply got dark, and the pressure on our ears turned to agony. The cliffs were great for diving off—at least my daredevil of an older brother thought so.

But my point in all this is that at this spot, that river represented these Spiritual Law. Yes, they are deep, but what you need is right there on the surface, clear to see.

There is no need to plumb the depth of the darkened water, to fight the agonizing pressure between one's ears, the confusion, darkness, and mental agony.

Chaos in life always accompanies the lies. They drag us down to where we can't see the truth in the laws. Hanging on to those lies is something we do to ourselves.

For all I've explained about it here, I expect that for some, the pressure between your own ears may be building with seeing the truth. When one is living a lie, the truth always demands change—change is scary.

Questions:
- Can you open your mind to truth?
- Do you feel like you've just been hit upside your head with a big stick? Unlike the one propping up your society's façade, this one has no shit covering it.

Action:
- ➤ This law is stated in simple terms. But as to its depth, likely you'll never see the bottom. Decide now to accept it as being the simple truth. But as to being in the realm of spirituality, it is as mystical as infinity.

Wet Farts

Y'know, there are those "come to Jesus" moments in life, those "realizations of divinity," as in your spirituality. And then there are those "welcome to your humanity" events as well.

Let's talk about these last ones. I recently ran across the picture of a woman on Facebook that was taken from a vantage point behind her. It showed that she'd recently had an accident in her pants. Nearly all Facebook comments were in jest—big fucking joke!

If your purpose here is to uplift yourself to your higher consciousness, that is impossible to do for those who are busy laughing at someone's pain.

Most found that picture hilarious. Even I, myself, would have at a time in my past. But the fact is that humanity, as a whole, is conditioned to find humor in the unthinkable things that might have or possibly sometime will happen to you, *yourself*. Our humor often is unconsciously used to help us get past the pain or sorrow in our lives.

Have you never had a wet fart? Do you think you might at some point in life? Embarrassing, don't you think? But let's look at the true reality of life, the spiritual reality of it.

In general, practically no one has a problem watching you eat. Food nourishes our bodies and moves on through. That end part is where we, due to our weak-minded, prejudicial judgments, do have a problem—it sounds bad and smells worse.

But when it is just ourself, sitting on the pot, playing tunes with our ass and stinking up our personal private bathroom, NO problem, right? Because it is us, we accept it as part of our humanity. But of someone else? *Unacceptable!*

Why is that? Why do we automatically go to, "My humanity is *okay*—yours is *not*"? And why do we generally laugh and make jokes about the type of thing in her picture? Is humor always the best way of handling the pain? Why not go straight to the empathy.

Can we visualize ourselves as ever being in that situation, or do we actually need to have been there? Would that stop the desire to see ourselves as being above it by mocking and humiliating others?

NOW . . . would you now laugh at this woman's pain? It is, after all, how our society has taught us all to be.

Questions:

- Valid question: Would you now laugh and belittle this woman?
- How about just her picture of it?
- Does the stink of someone else's shit bother you?
- How about your own should someone else get a whiff of it?

Actions:

- What would you do if you found yourself standing behind her in the drug store checkout line?
- Have your thoughts on it in any way changed? Write about it.
- Do you view the thought—or smell—of shit any differently? Write about that, too.

On the Road Less Travelled

Ah, "the road less travelled." It's really just the inner journey, the one so few people ever take. You see, being less travelled, it is full of potholes, unseen tree roots, and boulders one must get over or around. It's not a road one can take in their limo or even on their all-terrain cycle. Those obstacles are all composed of the things you have been told about life and believe but which are not true . . . lies you cannot see without help. That help comes in knowing life's real truths—the Spiritual Laws.

Then there's the truth discovered in your relationship with your significant other, who puts your shit right in your face. When you don't like the stink of it, that's just your soul's way of saying, "Look at this! There's something here about you that you need to see." That is when you need to apply those laws. They will point out your truth.

Sheeee-ttt! Those lessons are the real purpose of relationships. Love is just the icing. Sad how few ever learn through love. Most are too busy trying to control one another. Control is *never* love.

Me? I got a double whammy of help. Some from my wife, of course. She was very good at rubbing shit. But more so, it came from the Specter of Death. He's the one who taught me about the Spiritual Laws. Those laws then showed me what stunk up my life.

This book, this journey you are about to take, is similar to a book titled *The Secret* by <u>Rhonda Byrne</u>. Based on Spiritual Law, that book gives you an excellent view of life's truth. But there are far more secrets to know. With the Angel of Death offering it up, my life became *The Secret* on steroids. How could it be otherwise?

I've ridden motorcycles most of my life. As mentioned, this book begins in an ICU. That is not the place one would ever want to crash into in life, but it is the place from which I began my journey. Funny thing—it was not my motorcycle that set me on this road less travelled. It was my wife and an almost nonexistent little streak of shit.

Questions:
- How long have you traveled on this road?
- Have you discovered how the road gets easier, sometimes even enjoyable, the farther you go?

Action:
- ➤ Instead of slogging along, try dancing.

>>><<<

Ah, the Price!

There is this thing that I often do throughout this series of books—I repeat myself. Yes, often. I do this for a reason. You see, these *Redneck Spirituality* books are numbered in the order that they would best be read.

Still, they are separately published works. There will be those who will pick one up out of order. For the most part, it doesn't matter, and yet, there are certain lessons that must be learned.

As for humanity, we tend to skip over those lessons to which we have the most resistance. Just something we all do. But because those lessons are the ones that bring function to the dysfunction of our lives, they are the most important ones.

This particular lesson has been mentioned repeatedly in the other books. Here it is in the nut sack of life.

The things I write about here are those that I've learned about life, uncommon things that most people don't know. I write about it as a gift to you. Aside from the price you paid for the book, there is no further price levied by me. Not even the expectation that you will accept what I have to say.

However, one should never be willing to accept a gift when not knowing the cost of that gift . . . the pig in a poke thing.

Little piggies are cute, but even little piggies shit—a lot! And that shit will stink. That shit is what has nourished your little piggy. And who knows? That little piggy may yet nourish you, too.

This lesson is about understanding the price of living by these Spiritual Laws. So, I'll begin with recapping one of those laws for you.

Spiritual Law #5:

> *The Universe always balances. For every painfully unhappy thing that comes to your life, if you will but look, you will find a gift for which you can be grateful. Just so, those gifts you receive that give you joy will always be accompanied by something that will not.*

But wait! I thought that true gifts, like the gift of love, never carry a price, never have expectations attached.

Yes, that is so . . . between us mortals here in this world. But God's gifts to you are never gifts. They are lessons delivered by that part of you that is most actually of God—your soul. That is the totality of what this life, this world, is all about. Lessons! Therein lies the balance. The gift of every painful lesson is in the joy derived from lessons learned.

Now comes the zinger. Knowing these Spiritual Laws, these simple truths of life that make your life work so functionally, also carries a price. To know that price, to see it, requires you to be aware of the lies that fuck up the lives of everyone who does not know what you now do.

You know those lies because likely you, too, once believed them. They were the rules by which you ran your life—the lies of humanity's "normal" society. This is the price to you. You have now been nourished by a little truth. Those who believe the lies find the truth repugnant. And you? You now stink of pig shit to those "normal" people.

Questions:
- Did you ever try to share any of the Spiritual Laws (simple truths) with your "normal" friends?
- Did they resist it? Maybe call YOU out as being the dumbass?
- Did they wrinkle up their nose in disgust while doing that? Yeah—pig shit!

Actions:
- ➢ The only action I can suggest is this—be AUTHENTIC! If you worry about how others see you, you can NEVER be authentic.
- ➢ Besides, all you can do is offer your own thoughts and experiences, realizing THEY are the ONLY ones who have the right to change their mind.

Who Am I to Be Telling You Shit?

Who exactly am I to be telling you all this? A writer, a poet, a personal life coach, a philosopher. I've been all that. Some might judge me as being just some wacko. I am, well . . . different.

But as for who you see me as, that is merely a figment of your personal perception. No offense, but I really don't give a shit. The shit that's in your mind, stinky or not, is none of my business.

When I first meet someone, they quickly become aware that I am "not normal." I see it in their eyes, and it no longer bothers me. In fact, I regard it as a compliment.

Then when they find out I write books, they always ask what they are about. Ah, now that is the question. Do I tell them about those two novels—an autobiography—or memoirs? Essentially, it's my true story with a little attitude and way too much information.

Seems like a reasonable place to start. After all, my other books all follow that same venue. In admitting my truths, some might call it uncommon courage, or maybe uncommon knowledge—hell, possibly even insanity. In truth, it's merely what naturally follows when one comes face-to-face with their mortality and has nowhere to go except to step through their fears, or give up on life. Maybe even use those fears to teach others about life.

In opening its life to its own magnificence, does a butterfly have courage—or was it just the best choice? So it was with me.

One death, one birth. That is the story of that first book, *The Courage of a Butterfly.*

For me, this life began in that ICU at the age of forty-five with a massive blood clot on my lung—the kind few survive. Lying there with that fist clutching the inside of my chest, I was fully aware that any moment could be my last.

An unseen presence permeated that ICU, an awareness like smoke wafting through the room. Was it just the reality of my mortality? Who knows, but I knew that death was present, a tactile presence I could not deny.

With it came the realization that all the little lies I bullshitted myself about just to make my life work in the moment were no longer applicable. One does not tell lies when in the presence of the Angel of Death. Yes, that was when I died.

When the picture you hold as being who you are changes, your consciousness changes. And face it, what is death but a change in consciousness? This death was not the one I was expecting. Nonetheless, who I was did, indeed, die in that ICU.

You see, among those little lies was one big one—one with which I could no longer live.

Somewhere deep in my psyche, I'd always known that should that lie ever come into the light in my consciousness, it would surely obliterate who I was in life. It was not that blood clot that killed me in that life, it was that lie.

To die and be born on the same day . . . yes, that is the story that book tells. What is normal for a butterfly requires uncommon courage from mankind. Death is death, the ultimate about that which man is most afraid—the ultimate change. Courage is about stepping through your fear.

Earth is our schoolground, the place where our souls give us the lessons we need to grow and evolve. Everything we dislike that does us no actual harm just pisses us off. These are the ways in which these lessons are presented.

But our main motivational factor? That would be fear.

When we stop stepping through it and learning, what motivation does our soul then have to waste its time teaching this coward who is afraid to learn? It is the soul that holds our reset button for this life, y'know?

Questions:
- Have you ever thought about that—you know, that button?
- Have you ever been there, at the bottom of the cesspool of your life?
- You must not have given up—you ARE still here. But are you now wondering why your soul didn't just push the button?
- Hey, I don't mean to pull on your chain, but by now, are you wondering if this book is the last link holding you to life?

Action:
- ➤ If it were, what would be your next move? MAKE IT!

>>><<<

Soul's Lessons

No one gets out of this life alive. Some don't even realize that you do get out of it consciously. Are the things I write about the things you don't know? Will you want to know them when that time comes for you?

I write because not everyone will have the time to learn these things when it comes time to go. Death often comes as a surprise. It did for me, but then, I'm one of the lucky few who knew he didn't know shit but wanted to learn.

Maybe that is why I received a reprieve. You might consider my writings as your own reprieve before the fact. Will it show you that you, too, don't know shit? Thing is, this shit that I offer . . . do you want it?

It is your soul's job to teach you what it wants to experience in this lifetime. Your soul already knows everything, but you don't really "know" a thing without experiencing it.

You can get that experience firsthand—the hard way. Or, if you are open enough to what I show you in my writing about mine, if it touches you, that is the easy way.

Even so, it may only be preparing you with true knowledge by making you aware of the lies that, right now, are running your life.

Then . . . perhaps you will be ready to experience it firsthand for yourself. I will tell you about life's simple truths—the Spiritual Laws. Knowing them, and living them, will give you the experience needed for the easy way.

Questions:
- No, I am NOT telling you that you are stupid. I'm saying that like ALL "normal" people, we tend to believe what we are told as children, how that is the way this world

works. Few of us ever question it. Do you? Are you now willing to look?

- How fucked up will your world need to get before you will?
- Oh, it isn't? You are aware that this book in your hand IS a self-help book, right?

Actions:

➤ Open your mind and continue reading.

➤ You don't want to piss off your soul—or do you?

The Important Shit

What is this whole thing called the Universe, or creation? For something to be, doesn't it involve a creation, even a Creator? Otherwise, isn't it all just a chaotic jumble of everything?

And everything? Scientists say everything is energy, in some form or other. But scientists also say that there are rules—laws—regarding everything.

The laws of physics, laws of thermodynamics, gravity. You get the picture. Doesn't it mean that some incomprehensible intelligence must be making those rules, if only to bring it all from chaos to give it all some sort of functionality?

That essential intelligence is what mankind has always labeled as his God's. I submit that there must be but one God, if there would be anything other than chaos. Hell, surely there would be disagreements. After all, the Bible talks about God being jealous, judgmental, punishing . . . even says that we are made in God's image. Yeah, that is what we'd do. In fact, what we do all the time. No. Surely, there can't be more than one such being.

But what do I know? I'm only speculating on what those in authority, religion-wise, are telling me.

Smaller minds, such as mankind's, would most likely place that Supreme Being out there, somewhere, maybe in a place called heaven. Maybe they'd even pattern God as being someone who looks like himself, but is more magnificent. That IS what they are saying, isn't it?

Me? I don't think mankind does God justice. Surely, He/She/It is a much Higher Power—one way beyond man's petty bullshit. And seeing as everyone is familiar with the term "God," that is the one I generally use. It's short and sweet. "Higher Power," if used too often, would be repetitious, even boring. To me, that Higher Power is anything but boring.

As for the rules, the laws? I have to look to the ones governing life. Those, it seems, are where most folks want to make up their own rules—rules that serve only themselves and, therefore, aren't true for everyone.

But I am different from most folks. You see, there was that time when I was not expecting to live. It's a quandary. Maybe it's nuts, but I do believe I did, indeed, die. The man who went into that ICU was not the same man who came out.

No one comes out of this life alive. Me? I came out of that ICU with a burning desire that when next there comes the time to die, I would be someone I liked and respected. But to be that in life requires one to know oneself. For that, one needs to know the truth of life—in particular, one's own.

So, what is the truth of life, everyone's life? Since that time, I have discovered a great deal about that. I don't write these books just to tell my story. Everyone has their own.

I have written two novels about my life. In them, I use my story to illustrate these truths. I wrote them so that you could relate them to your own life—but only IF you want to.

One thing that shook me to my core in that ICU was seeing that my whole life, up to that point, meant nothing, added nothing to this world. THAT is why I write.

Feel free to take what YOU need and leave the rest. I am NOT a preacher or guru. I lay NO expectations on you. Instead, I ask that you do your own FUCKING thinking.

Did that F-bomb blow up in your face? It was meant to. I am a redneck, and that is the redneck way of pointing out the important shit. Was my redneck wording offensive to you? Oh well, FUCK me. No one is forcing you to read.

Giving you your life's lessons is YOUR soul's purpose, not MINE. Getting your anus in a pucker is often the way your soul says, "Pucker up, Buttercup, this is something you need to hear."

Questions:
- Do you find my language offensive? I can see why a "gentleman" might go there.
- Me? I'm too honest to wear the façade of a gentleman—you DO see that as a façade, don't you?
- On a scale from "just a little chapped" to a "full pucker," where is your ass sitting on it right now?

Action:
- ➤ In reading this book, "not chapped at all" is what you want to shoot for.

>>><<<

Judgments and Duality

Again, this world is one of duality. Everything has a from and a to, a beginning and an end, a like and a dislike, a good and an evil, a right and a wrong, and a loving and an unloving. GET IT? Our world is comprised entirely of OUR OWN perceptions—the span of our judgments.

That's right, the judgmental shit from between our own ears. No one judges everything the same. And no one has the right to wipe their judgments—the shit from between their ears—off on anyone else.

The truth of this existence is that "out there," there is no good or evil. Nothing is right or wrong. The world "out there" is a physical construct. Our own world "in here" is a mental construct, one that differs from everyone else's—in here.

Therein lies our personal power in life. We get to see the world out there in any way we like. And because it is a physical world, all of it is comprised of energy in one form or other. It is, therefore, a spiritual experience because we are also made of that energy. But more so, our energy of life is sentient. Self-aware, self-creative—all of life is a spiritual experience for ourselves.

And MORE:

It will come to us exactly as we see it. Yes, it's our free choice to make our personal worlds as perfect as we want . . . or not.

Being sentient, we are the peak of it—the conscious, creative part of it all, the God consciousness part of that Higher Power. Some may be more conscious than others, but we ALL are an actual part of the infinity called God.

And yes, I AM AWARE that I am repeating this concept one more time. Can ya hear me now?

Questions:

- Okay, pretty much every religious person is going to have an issue with this one. Do you?
- It seems that for those who see themselves as deeply religious, it is only because they have burrowed themselves into their religion very deeply and are clinging. Have you?
- You might not like this next question. Maybe it doesn't NEED to be asked. It isn't MY

  need, although it might be yours. That's why I'm asking it anyway. How much longer are you going to be like a tick clinging to the ass end of organized religion?

Actions:

- ➤ Keep on reading, and when you're done, then make that determination. It is not my intent to wreck your faith in God.
- ➤ It IS my intent to teach you to do your own FUCKING thinking.
- ➤ Maybe even to bolster your belief in that Higher Power more than your religion now does. You know how in order to keep horses from being distracted by traffic, they used to put blinders on them when pulling the milk cart? I'm asking you take yours off for a short time to see what you can see.

It Is Not "Out There"

There is rude and there is crude. Rude is a judgment call on your part. Coming from a place of self-superiority, crude is more of a judgment call on society's part. Being a redneck, I've been called both.

What someone does or says—who they are being—is simply "what is" and doesn't demand judgment. The fucked-up part is about that sense of superiority that is often between a person's or persons' ears. It doesn't exist in the world "out there," in reality.

The reality of this world is what is termed "the truth." What someone says or does—a word or gesture—is just that. We supply our own meaning to it. Our judgments need to be reserved for the proper place in life, for the real questions. Is it actually harmful to anyone's physical life or being? If it is, that is the thing that must be judged and addressed.

Beyond that, beyond what is between someone's ears? The question needs to only concern the energy. Is the energy loving or something not loving?

Fear is simply a little lizard sent by one's soul to warn against possible danger. We are the ones who blow it up into a dragon using the winds of possibility. Just so, harsh feelings are the soul's simple messages sent to warn of a possible minor dysfunction in our life. We are the ones who blow it up into something hideous by blaming our feelings on someone else.

Questions:

- Is there anything you have taken offense with in this book?
- Do you realize THAT thing is pointing to a dysfunction your soul wants you to deal with?

Action:

➢ Deal with it.

What Pisses You Off

It's the things that really piss you off that are the most telling. You see, it is your choice to like or not like something. It's really quite simple. Those things you don't like merely raise the question—why?

Then there are those who piss you off. Again, why? But this "why' is the one you are most likely to lie to yourself about. Could that be because of what you know is the truth?

Truth is, you don't like it because what they are saying is the truth. It's your soul that is pissed off. No one's soul takes something kindly when you feel the need to lie. You lie because you know your thinking is fucked up. Your soul knows it, too.

That you're lying to yourself completely blows your soul's lesson out of the water. Everyone's soul is pissed when you're sinking your own ship.

Questions:
- Has there ever been a time when, being pissed off, you weren't blaming your choice of feelings on someone or something else?
- What if your soul was actually demanding that you look at something about yourself and your thinking?
- Are you going to run that thought across your mind the next time you are pissed?

Actions:
- ➢ Don't be that pissed-off little woosy who won't take responsibility for his or her simple choice of feelings.
- ➢ For the first time in your life, be someone your soul can respect.
- ➢ Consider this: What if your soul is the part of that Higher Power you face when you die? Kinda personal, ain't it?

>>><<<

The Ten Commandments

The Ten Commandments List, Short Form

> *1. Thou shall have no other Gods before me.*
> *2. Nor make graven images.*
> *3. Thou shalt not take the name of the Lord thy God in vain.*
> *4. Thou shalt remember the Sabbath day and keep it holy*
> *5. Thou shalt honor thy father and thy mother.*
> *6. Thou shalt not commit murder.*
> *7. Thou shalt not commit adultery.*
> *8. Thou shalt not steal.*
> *9. Thou shalt not bear false witness against thy neighbor.*
> *10. Thou shalt not covet thy neighbor's goods nor his wife.*

The first three show God not as **all-powerful**, but rather as insecure. But remember, *what we see in others is but the reflection of ourselves.*

The fourth is good stewardship of the people. Everyone needs a break. The last six are not about *you* so much as how you treat others—common sense.

I'm not saying they are right or wrong. As far as the guidance the people needed at the time, they served very well.

Which begs the question: Have we not changed? Do we still need God to make these same demands on us? Do those first three still validate our own insecurities?

The fourth gives us all a break for resting and to worship God. The break part is good sense, but worshipping God? I don't think an all-powerful God needs our worship. But we? Maybe we need to see our own insignificance in it all in order not to look down on others. After all, isn't it human nature to wipe our shit off on those we see as below us?

I'm saying "Look up, not down" We are the ones who need to see something greater than ourselves.

Benefit of the doubt—maybe God is just reminding us of our connection to Him/Her/It, and our responsibility to own our lives. That is much better than allowing us to blame others when our own shit stinks.

The last six . . . yeah, how we treat others is only common sense. Our society doesn't have a whole lot of that.

So, okay. "Chu *still* gotta lotta growin' to do, esse." And me? Seeing it is a far cry short of doing it.

Questions:
- Do you think I'm belittling The Ten Commandments? I'm not.
- Do you think that like now, back then, their society wasn't equally fixated on teaching people to see themselves as insecure victims?
- Do you remember the reasons why that is and has always been so?

Actions:
- ➢ If you don't remember, go back and do some rereading. This is possibly the greatest concept this book has to offer.
- ➢ And no, I do believe these Ten Commandments are still applicable. Mankind hasn't changed much. Consider that.
- ➢ But I am different . . . not good, not bad, not better than, just different. Knowing the Spiritual Laws—life's truths—has indeed shown me a different view. This last page was an explanation of just how my view differs from most. Ponder that as you read on through this book.

The Energy

What I want to offer you here is an understanding of what these Spiritual Laws mean in life—how they show up and how they make a difference.

Let's start with this question: What if there were no right or wrong? And more to the point, why do we insist on having the belief that they do exist "out there" in THE world for everyone? And why are they coated with such stickiness that our minds get so stuck to them, it's almost impossible to let go.

To understand my point, you'll need to see it in the light of the Spiritual Laws—again, the simple truths. Right and wrong exist only between your own ears. Like good and bad, they are merely your judgments. They are NOT the same for everyone.

Kinda throws a different light on this judgmental society and its lies. Doesn't that make you wonder why we all go there? Why does how I see *my* life have to be the same as you in *yours*?

Instead of using the judgmental lies our society has taught us as being "the law," let's use a different set of categories. How about *what is—what is the truth* and *what isn't? Therein lies what works—and what doesn't.*

And then there is the ultimate category: *What is loving* and *what is not.* This spells out how there is a choice to the energy in which everyone lives.

You are naturally going to form an opinion about everything that comes into your life. Many of those beliefs will be the truth of life. Most will not. And of those not, most will be the beliefs of others that you have accepted as your own—the lies that those you see as authorities have told you.

Why did they lie to you? Was it out of weakness? It is so much easier to blame others for your problems than to take responsibility. Most often, those problems are due to believing something to be true when it is not. Then, of course, there is how you feel about something and your inability to take responsibility for those feelings when a lie would serve to blame. Blame is *always* a lie.

It is your soul's job to give you your lessons in life. Those lessons are always about any lies we think of as being your personal truth. And that will always be about what you aren't willing to see and accept as being your responsibility.

This life is about you—no one else.

Ah, yes. Life seems so confusingly difficult. Funny when the truth is spelled out so clearly in the Spiritual Laws. They have been being written about for centuries. Being unwilling to accept responsibility, especially for your feelings, is where life gets fucked up. Those truths, these laws, are simply about your responsibilities in life.

Again, that is summed up in the very first law: *I am the Creator.* All you need do is learn the laws and accept the lessons of your soul.

It might help to know that the soul speaks with the language of emotion. The things you dislike are *always* pointing to your lessons. And the truth . . . the Spiritual Laws? Each book in this series offers you some of the laws. Book Four offers fifty-five of them. There are many more. I, too, am still learning.

Questions:
- Are you getting a clue about how the lies fuck up your life every time?

- Did repeating it in a different context this time help you understand?
- Do you believe that lies may sometimes be justified, even be loving, when they spare someone from facing their feelings?
- Isn't the truth really about you and your fear of being the bearer of bad news?
- Do you see that in the end, lies are always dysfunctional?

Actions:

- ➤ Dedicate your life to knowing the truth, especially when that truth may make you "wrong."
- ➤ Rejoice in seeing yourself as wrong. That alone tells you that your life has taken a huge step forward.

>>><<<

Beings of Energy

We are all beings of energy inhabiting this body. Your soul is the highest level of your energy, the part that actually connects you with the Higher Power. The Higher Power is the intelligence that runs the Universe—God, for lack of a better term. As part of God's infinite knowledge, your soul knows everything.

But knowing a thing intellectually falls short of knowing the full gamut of it by physically experiencing it. That is our purpose here in this world, where everything has a beginning and an end. In that Higher Power's world—the world where your soul resides—that world is infinite. It has no beginning, no end.

Your soul—your personal part of God—put you here to get experience. You are the part of infinity that experiences life. Did God need to dum-dum everyone's consciousness in order to even get such experience? I suspect so. What do YOU think, DUMMY?

Questions:
- If you were conscious of everything your soul knows, would you want to gain the experience?
- Remember how that experience runs the full gamut—the part that feels good through to the part that does not?

Action:
- ➢ Which part do you think your soul will focus on and appreciate the most? The rest just makes that part feel even better. Rejoice in what that means, DUMMY.

Like a Square Peg

What you know is always limited, but what you don't know is limitless. That Higher Power most call God knows everything, creates everything, is within everything, and everything is limitless. Everything is infinite.

So, God is infinite. We can define infinity, but we cannot "know" infinity. Just so, we cannot "know" God. We can only experience that Higher Power inasmuch as we experience ourselves. We are part of everything—of God.

But in this worldly plane, everything has a beginning and an end.

For us, knowing God is limited here to knowing one's self, the full gamut. But in this life, we cannot fully know our soul. We only get that after we are dead and can experience the infinite limitlessness of our soul.

We are an actual part and piece of God. What we can know of God while here in this worldly existence is limited to what we can experience of ourselves. Knowing the Higher Power in our head—the concept of God—is limited to our inner experience of who we, ourselves, are. Perhaps that is why Socrates said, "The unexamined life is not worth living."

Again, in order to fully know **God, the Higher Power,** one does need to pass over the vail into **that higher realm.**

But then there are a few, like myself, who have been graced with the view from the precipice and are changed. Like a square peg in a round hole, I no longer quite fit, nor do I quite "know."

To have one's life burnt down to the embers, to the truth of who one is, has been an awesome experience. But the Phoenix is a lonely bird. Is that why this Universe, this almighty God, is so bent on creating life in its every possible form—companionship?

Does knowing these Spiritual Laws put me one step closer to the Almighty? Certainly, I am "not normal." Is that why I too, have a craving for companionship? Is it the price I pay?

To die someone I like and respect—isn't that what I wanted back then in that ICU? The price . . . is worth it.

Questions:
- Do you suppose we supply companionship for God?
- Or maybe we supply entertainment, what with all our silly little traumas and dramas?
- Maybe it is all that and more?
- Life, especially sentient life, must be very precious to God. D'ya think?
- If so, just playing a sentient part in the theater of eternity is precious to me. It is all I have. How about you?

Action:
- ➢ Go and play your part with excellence. Do it with all of the love you can muster.

Stand Alone

Writing this series of books on Spiritual Laws has been a challenge. You see, these books are presented with the easier concepts first. They then get deeper with each book. Nevertheless, there is no guarantee that they will be read in that order.

This one, Book Five, is by far the deepest. And yet, they MUST all be capable of standing on their own. It is the same for us in our personal life.

I've been sprinkling a few of the simpler laws into this section by way of catching you up to speed and making it more understandable. They are the parts in *bold italics*. The Spiritual Laws section comes next and will go into it with more depth.

Me? In writing this series, I have been constantly amazed when realizing how much I DIDN'T know about life in general, and mine in particular. In the time since that ICU, I've often wondered why my soul didn't push my reset button sooner.

Everything happens for a reason. And as for our soul's lessons, when we refuse to learn them, they just get harder the next time they're presented.

Questions:
- How willing have you been lately in learning your soul's lessons?
- Is it possible your soul is fingering YOUR reset button, RIGHT NOW?

Action:
- ➤ Just a thought. Consider it.

New Thought—The Philosophy

Okay, maybe to begin, I need to step back and clarify a few things. Like, what is this New Thought philosophy all about?

It's really simple. While based on a Higher Power—God—it is *not* about religion. New Thought is based on the simple truths of life that, like gravity, "just are" and always hold true. No exceptions.

Why are they generally known as "Spiritual Laws"? Simple. Because they revolve around a Higher Power that is, and always has been, what created this Universe as well as the rules that make it all work.

Religions? The difference is that religions are created by man wishing to claim the power of God as his own for the purpose of controlling his fellow man. Religions—all the ones I know—are about power and control. About one man convincing others that he knows God better, and that he knows what God wants from everyone. Truth is, he is a thief, stealing that power. And us? We are the dumb fucks who hand it over to him.

How am I any different? I don't want power or control. I only want truth and understanding of something that I recognize is beyond my comprehension, except on a very limited basis. So, I take what I know of these simple basic truths and look deeper.

So why me? What gives me the ability to tell you anything? Put like that, I'll just say that I was given a gift from death, of looking at life in the imminence of death. From that precipice, at the end of it all, I will always see life from a place few ever get to look. And even fewer are then given some time to see the truth.

I'm going to take that thought, that flight of fancy, and get reeee-ul fancy with it. Let's begin with the truth of all life in this great big Universe. Let's push the boundaries of it.

Do you believe it's true that everywhere life can exist, given the infinity of time available to that Higher Power, God, it WILL exist—well . . . eventually?

Now, why do you think the Creator is so bent on creating life? And what is the peak of that life? Sentience maybe? Thinking, creating, self-aware intelligence?

Would you admit that for this particular world, that would likely be us—you and me? Why? Why would God be so bent on creating life? And we being the upper echelon, the crust, on it locally. WHY? What purpose do we have in the grand scheme of God?

Do you think God was just lonely? Or bored? Again, I'm sure what with all our silly dramas, we probably could act as the entertainment for the theater of eternity. Maybe? Maybe it's all that, but don't cha think there's gotta be more . . . much more?

The Bible talks about how God is omnipotent—everywhere, everywhen, within everything, including us. How we are an actual part of God. Remember that? Well, God doesn't make shit just for the stink of drama. Or does He?

Taking a step back and looking at it, God is infinite—no beginning, no end. So maybe this world is indeed like a theater to Him. This world is binary, remember. Everything has a beginning and an end.

Maybe this world is where God goes to stretch Himself through His experience of our binary lives. Here, there is a beginning and an end to everything, the full-gamut sweet to sour thing. Even to our thinking, good to evil, right to wrong, loving to not loving.

Whoa! Could it be that most of the binary-ness of this world stems from our thinking, our petty judgments?

I suspect this IS a special place for God and why we are also special. After all, what is the purpose that we fill for God? Aren't we the part of Him that experiences life? I like to see us as being the tastebuds of God. The simple truth about it for us is that we can't "know" a thing until we move it from between our ears and put it in our hearts.

That takes experience, the full gamut, the "from and to" experience. So, it makes sense that we would be the part of God that experiences life.

Question:
- Do you realize that while our physical existence is binary, it is likely where mankind takes it all into our judgmental minds . . . that it makes our sentient experience also binary, through emotions?

Action:
- ➢ More on that later. WATCH FOR IT. When you see it, come back and write about it.

The Simple Truths of Life

I started out here telling you about some specific Spiritual Laws. I've since decided that is not what I want to discuss here. Hell, I just finished writing a four-book series on that. If you are interested in me and what I've said so far about it, you can get books one through four. Right now, I want to dig deeper into what those laws mean in life—how they show up, and how they make a difference in the true-life experience of being human.

So again, let's go back to that question: *What if there were no right or wrong?* And more to the point, why do we insist on having the belief that they do exist in life anywhere outside of being a judgmental label we put on it?

To see my point, you'll need to view it in the light of Spiritual Law, which is simply the real truth. Again, "right and wrong," like "good and bad," are merely your judgments.

Kinda throws a different light on this judgmental society and its lies. Doesn't that make you wonder why we all go there? And why does everything in *my* life, to me, have to look the same as in *your* life, to you?

Instead of using the judgmental lies that our society has taught us to see everything as being, let's use a different set of categories that involve "what is" — what is the truth and what isn't? The truth is found only in the beliefs that work.

But then there is the ultimate category: "What is loving and what is not?" Therein lies the energy in which everyone lives.

> *Yes, I know I've already covered this. I'm repeating it*
> *only because it is so "not normal" to see these concepts*
> *in the lives of most "normal" people.*

You are naturally going to form an opinion about everything that comes into your life. Many of those beliefs will be the truth of life. Again, most will not. And of those not, most will be the beliefs of others whom you see as authorities. They told you, and you have accepted their beliefs as your own. Just so, many are lies that they, too, unconsciously came to believe about the world. *Truth is, we have all been trained NOT to see the truth.* Do I need to repeat this again?

Why? Is it out of your fear or theirs? If they can control your beliefs, they can control you. If so, then they don't need to fear that you will discover the real truths.

Fear, and the struggle to control one another that it then inspires . . . this is the sickness all mankind suffers from, and all of it is based on a lie. The truth is, we can only actually control ourselves. We control others only inasmuch as they will let us. Can you see the lie?

How long do you think man has suffered under these sick, fucking lies? *Forever . . . maybe.* Insanity is doing the same thing over and over and expecting a different result. Believing that you control what you do not . . . would that be insanity or stupidity—or maybe both?

Could it be unconscious because they, too, have been taught to believe it about themselves? Do they lie to you just to get you believing that you aren't in control of your life? Is this a necessary step for them to be in control—a step most take from an unconscious level of the mind?

Is it out of weakness, it being so much easier to blame others for your problems than to take responsibility? Most often, those problems are due to how you feel about something— your inability to take responsibility for those feelings when a lie would serve to blame them on others. Blame is *always* a lie.

It is your soul's job to give you your lessons in life. Those lessons are always about what the truth is. Your personal truth may vary some, but Spiritual Law truths don't. And that will always be about what you aren't willing to look at and accept as being your responsibility.

This life is about you—no one else.

Ah, yes. Life seems so confusingly difficult. Funny when the truth has been spelled out so clearly in the Spiritual Laws for centuries. The truth is eternal, y'know?

Being unwilling to accept responsibility, especially for your feelings, is where every person alive gets their life fucked up. These truths—these Spiritual Laws—are simply about your responsibilities in life.

Again, that is summed up in the very first law: *I am the Creator.* All you need do is learn the laws and accept the lessons of your soul.

It might help to know that the soul speaks with the language of emotion. The things you dislike are always pointing to your lessons. And the truth ... the Spiritual Laws? Each of the *Redneck Spirituality* books offers you some of the laws. Book Four offers fifty-five of them. There are many more. I, too, am still learning them.

Question:
- Have you read any of Books One through Four?

Action:
- ➤ Get them and read. You will not have the ability to fully understand some of what is in this book without them.

At the End of Life

Ah, the buffet table at the end of life, to look at and finally see all the lies I believed were truth—truths that my life was based upon. And to have the stench of all that shit I thought was nourishing me clogging my nostrils.

There is nothing like an Angel of Death to point out the truths of life—truths too inconvenient for me to see back then.

Dreadfully inconvenient, knowing that the cost of looking took all the comfort of familiarity from my life and demanded change.

And so, all those years were spent stumbling through life on the broken bones of those dysfunctional lies, the truth of which demanded that most frightful thing in life—CHANGE!

Ah, but to follow through requires more courage than I believed I had. The cost of all that change? Do you have what it takes to meet it in your own life?

Seeing it, and doing it now, could be the greatest gift ever offered by your soul. If you don't do it now, what remains is but to beg a reprieve of the Angel. That Angel doesn't give very many, y'know?

It is not the morals of others describing what is right and true for them, but rather, the morals of one's own personal sense of truth. For me, that was gleaned from what meeting the Angel has meant to my life.

But then there is the stench of that elephant dump of shit on the table of life. Right now, all the truth the Angel offers comes as simply a small packet of seeds—seeds from which change will grow.

Will it grow weeds with thorns to terrorize life with pain? Do you have the courage to cast them forth and accept the truth of all that grows from the "what is" of life?

I did. I cast them into that disgusting shit I once thought nourished my life. Nourished? Now it nourishes the magnificence of all that is true and holy, the essence of which now is of beauty to my sight, and of the sweetness tickling my senses with the true fragrance of my being.

Society told me I would only be acceptable to others when wearing the pink paint of society's shitty façade. It was never "others" to whom I needed to be acceptable, but only to myself. Again, the table of my life now holds an endless bouquet of my life's sweetness.

Acceptance—acceptance of what is the truth of life—is all that is needed to negate the pain of what is not.

Questions:
- Yeah, sounds kinda esoteric. Are you seeing the hard truth yet?
- You, too, just might find yourself getting naked in front of the whole world, like me now. Y'think?

Action:
- ➤ Think about what all this series has to offer. Then consider writing your own damn book.

Do Your Own Fucking Thinking

Life boils down to your beliefs. Seeing yourself as the next Evil Knievel or Spider Man will certainly give excitement to your life—if they are your truths, and if you can deal with broken bones. But the easier, more functional way is to see life itself in light of the truth. Changing your thoughts is so much easier and functional than changing your actions.

Personal growth only works with the discovery of truth—the truth of your own real physical abilities, or the truth of your life's real beliefs, but TRUTH.

So how do you discover truth? You can walk under a flock of seagulls to discover their truth, but if you are doing your own fucking thinking, you WON'T.

Going through life believing everything you are told, believing that other people know more than you, is the same as walking around under a flock of seagulls. You will discover the truth of it by getting shit on.

It's good to know that these Spiritual Laws you are always the simple truths of life, don't cha think?

Question:
- Are you beginning to see what these truths will mean to your life?

Action:
- ➢ GO! See what you can see.

The Bar of Humanity

Spiritual Laws—can't say it enough— are simply the things of life that always hold true. They are the clean functionality of life itself and couldn't be that without being true.

Perhaps the best thing about knowing these truths is that then you can see the lies. Most people live their entire lives without knowing what you now do.

You can expect your whole life will change. Your perception of it has changed. Your perception IS your world.

You are now "NOT NORMAL"!

Exhilarating, isn't it? You are not better than other people. It is just that mankind, in his/her own greed and need to control, has set the bar of humanity so very low and then anchored it down by the weight of lies—lies you no longer need to struggle under.

Questions:
- Will these laws hold joy for you?
- Or will they simply hold the fear of what all those changes will mean to your life?

Action:

> ➢ Have courage.

The Truth and Nothing But

We've all been trained to live in a box. The truth about this fucked-up box of humanity is that IT NORMALLY SUCKS. I'll say that again. "NORMAL" sucks! And once more, NO ONE gets to be EXTRAORDINARY by being NORMAL.

Our whole life, our religions, our society, even our parents have always been about that box called NORMAL. If you aren't in that box, you can't be controlled.

Why controlled? Because "NORMAL" is nothing more than the lies we've all been taught to believe. If you refuse to believe, but instead seek out the truth, you WILL change your whole world. And they, then, WILL have an opportunity to change theirs.

> *If you are living the truth, others*
> *will see it and want to live it, too.*

And YOU? You have to give up the comradery of that box and all aspects of being acceptable by those within. But YOU get to be exceptional. Exceptional is different, scary. Exceptional changes the world. YOU make a change in the world by truth. And truth makes it a better place.

Questions:

- What makes your truth any better than that of those in that box?
- Could it be that the truth is what resides in the real world—the world outside one's personal beliefs and perceptions—the world where TRUTH is the same for everyone?

- OMG! Is there really such a place?
- But in a world where everyone sees things the same, would it not then be boring?
- You are the Creator—REMEMBER?
- Creating your life from truth is functional. Can you agree?
- Does creating your life to be different based on the truth ever necessitate telling lies?
- Are there not a billion, maybe even infinite, aspects of truth?

Actions:
- ➤ Look up Spiritual Laws #41 and #42.
- ➤ Now, choose which energy you want to live by in your life—love or fear.

Sucking Society's Cock

Life . . .
That, and an unknown time to live it, is the bottom line of your existence here on Earth. So why would you allow every other greedy bastard in this thing called society to demand you to live your life their way?

Control . . .
That is the cock suck of our civilization. When you bow down on your knees to society and voluntarily live the way they demand, what does it get you? What then is the bottom line of your existence?

Acceptance . . .
Yes, acceptance and all the splooge you can swallow. Is it worth it?

Why . . .

Why is it needed? Your parents needed control in order to keep you safe and to keep you from being unloving to the other members of your family—and to give themselves time to teach you how to suck the cock of society.

Society . . .

Being members of their society, they then teach you society's rules—all you must do to become an acceptable cocksucker like they are. But they, and society, are lying.

Truth . . .

The truth they don't teach you about is love. What if they taught you to love, fully knowing that the acceptance of others only depends on your choice to love—to live your life to suit your soul, and to love.

Injury . . .

Physical injury to others is the bottom line of what is unloving and truly unacceptable.

Feelings . . .

That is where society fucks themselves. They refuse to take responsibility for their feelings. The main responsibility that we, as loving humans, have lies only where we have the ability to respond and to respond with love—first to your soul and then to others.

Responsibility . . .

You are the only one who has the ability to respond. You determine how you feel about everything. When you are loving, you need no control of others. Outside of physically protecting yourself, you need no control over anyone.

Sucking cock . . .

Do you need to live your life sucking the cock of society? The acceptance of others does depend on you giving them control—you living your life to suit them, YOU SUCKING THE COCK OF SOCIETY. Or is the truth simply that the acceptance of other loving souls is ONLY dependent on your being loving, too.

So, fuck . . .

Fuck society and its lying rules. Do you need the acceptance of those who would blame you for their feelings, allowing them to avoid the responsibility of being loving themselves? Or would you prefer the company of other responsible, loving souls, like yourself, who are not acceptable members of a cock sucking society?

Now . . .

Do you feel that what was said here is not acceptable to be said to you? Oh, you do? Then perhaps you are a card-carrying, acceptable member of society. Knowing that truth will never feel good to you.

Insanity . . .

Society demands you live by their rules. But when their rules are lies, then you must pretend to wear that façade of lies—IF you are an acceptable liar.

A Pretense . . .

Do you NOT see that society's acceptance is also a pretense, also a lie? If you refuse to live your life by society's beliefs—if you dare to think differently, to live by what is the truth of life—then you are labeled as insane.

My loneliness . . .

Every life is a whole spectrum thing. It takes the good and the bad, the joy and the sadness, my loneliness and my you. Why is it I didn't see you until now—now that we're through—me creating my life without you?

A gift . . .

Everyone in your life has a gift to give you. This IS a Spiritual Law, y'know. No matter how it all shakes out, YOU were there, THEY were there, and the GIFT was there, AND IT STILL IS. It is up to us to see that gift. Problem is that seeing and accepting are two different things. Some never see it . . . until YOU . . . are gone.

Gone . . .

Sometimes GONE is the necessary element for us to SEE and to ACCEPT the lesson.

Questions:

- Are you getting a sense of how society only serves itself? And how every facet of society does the same?
- Y'know, there's mothers' milk and then there's splooge. Mothers want to nourish their children. Do you get that splooge isn't all that nourishing? And society isn't nourishing anyone but itself?

Action:

- ➢ Do all your sucking at your mother's tit, not society's dick.

Judgmental Shit

If you have read the first four books in this series, it may not have been necessary to lay this shit off on you to familiarize you with a few of the laws. But if this is your first, then it was necessary to do in order for it to be a stand-alone read. The concepts of this Thought System are just that far outside the box.

In this Part Three, I've gone over the same concepts in every scenario possible ad nauseam! (If that isn't yet a real word, it deserves to be.)

Part Two offered you the Spiritual Laws alone. The *questions* and *actions* are there to encourage you to think for yourself.

All the parts yet to come will focus on specific areas of life, areas that most self-help books generally skirt lightly over or don't mention at all. They are those subjects we are all admonished NOT to talk about in public—Religion, Relationships, Sexuality, and Politics.

Together, they make up the deep end of the pool. They are the waters in which few people can let go of their judgments long enough to actually swim. They tie themselves to that anchor every time and will fight to make those beliefs float.

To prevent this from becoming just another cesspool of life, you may require copious amounts of toilet paper to keep your judgmental shit out of the water.

I'm talking about that *right or wrong, good or bad* judgmental shit that only exists between your ears and usually leaks out of your mouth, or explodes as diarrhea. I'm asking that you keep it honest, and clean, and real, like you have never done before.

This is NOT about organized religion and the evil children of Satan. It is NOT even about morality. Nor does it have anything that speaks to being a credit to your family, your community, or your society. No. This speaks to the reality of who we are—without society's fake, fucking façade.

This takes it down to the lowest common denominator of life: LOVING or UNLOVING.

What if we all were simply honest human beings who prefer to be loving. And can actually accept that you may not have the exact same beliefs as me. But we can interact, and share, and even enjoy this world in which we are all living.

PART FOUR
Religion

The ultimate Liberal way—
What better way for a man to slake his thirst for power than to
become a preacher—the broker—who distributes the power of
an almighty God?

Spirituality vs. Religion

It is the experience we all have of this world. Spirituality "just is." Nor does it require our awareness of a Higher Power—the one most habitually called "God." This, I believe, is so, as we essentially are a part of it all. Isn't God the thing that infuses all of creation, perhaps IS creation? God is, after all, considered to BE the Creator, right?

So, what is this thing called "religion?" And what does it have to do with God? I think it is simply man's attempt to use our awareness of that Higher Power—of God—to his own advantage.

Religion is GOOD, religion is BAD. In fact, religion could be looked at as the determining factor in all that is good and bad, and even what is evil. Religion is the JUDGMENTAL element where man sees himself above the others and uses their beliefs in God to advantage. Man is what is good . . . or evil. Religion, and its terms, are only man's judgments.

God, that Higher Power, is perfect—the perfection of all that is. Not GOOD, not BAD. It just IS—AND IT IS ALL GOD.

Mankind would do better to leave his judgments and God alone, to stop trying to use the power of the Universe to control others. You see, the term "LOVE" has not yet been mentioned. Despite what they say, religions have little to do with what love is, and a lot to do with what it is not.

Now consider: I just pissed off every religious person on Earth. Does "pissed off" come from a place of love? Just a thought. We are all entitled to have our own thoughts, you know—unless we are religious.

God, the Higher Power, made the Cosmos. He/She/It made it all. The Galaxies, the Star Systems, the Universes, Suns, Planets—everything from the macro to the micro and smaller, the infinitely large to the infinitesimally small. Is God the actual energy of it all, or does God, as many believe, fill the larger volume between the particles? I don't know. No one does.

It doesn't FUCKING matter what we know or believe where God is concerned. God is INFINITE, and we have not the capacity to truly know infinity.

But we do have the capacity to know who we are. We are a part and piece of it all—a part of God, Him/Her/Its self. As such, we have access to the power of God in the creation of our lives.

Though, on a much smaller scale, we are also sentient. Not nearly as much as God, but enough that how we can see our world—our personal world—as being. It will be exactly as we see it. And God, the all mighty, will allow it to come to us just so.

But we are afflicted with this thing called greed. WE WANT IT ALL. That is why mankind creates religions. It is man's way of stealing and wielding ALL the power of God against his fellow man for the purpose of power, of control.

Don't you see the sad reality of it all? YOU—ME—WE—are the ones who give him (or her) that power to wield. We do it because we don't have the courage to create our own lives. We are too FUCKING lazy to believe in ourselves and too STUPID to see that we aren't thinking (or creating) for ourselves. We don't need religion to do our thinking or to create our lives for us.

Hell, isn't it clear yet that men and women of religion are only creating for themselves? They do it by stealing your own personal, inalienable, God-given power.

Questions:
- Do you understand what I'm really saying about who and what we are?
- Or did I just confuse you—maybe piss you off?

Action:
➢ Keep on reading.

Like a Drop in the Ocean

Everything in this Universe is energy in one form or another, including us. We, physically, mentally, and spiritually, are a part of this Universe. And God? Don't most folks think of God as being omnipotent—everywhere, within everything? Sounds to me like that is saying God is the energy of it all, including us.

"WTF does that mean?" you might be asking me. Or maybe some of you are asking yourself: *Do I really want to follow this raving nutcase down into these depths?* Y'know, you could change that thought around to: *Do I really want to follow this lunatic up into these scary, rarified heights? I might just fall and break my head.*

Yup, you might, because what it all means is just this: YOU are an actual part of and piece of God. Read Laws #20, #30, and #31. Like a drop in the ocean of God—or as Rumi said back in the thirteenth century: ". . . the ocean in a drop." That's exactly so. YOU are more powerful than most folks can even conceive because YOU have access—*you are part of the power of God.* They can't see it in you because they don't see it in themselves.

Did anyone here ever see the movie or read the book, *The Secret?* It is also about the Spiritual Laws. It describes how that power works, but on a surfacy, gimme-gimme sort of way. You might consider looking it up. With me, you are going deeper—or higher. You decide.

I suspect I am about to lose a significant part of the churchgoing crowd. Most religions would have you see yourself as being separate from God up there, while being part of the flock down here. I am not looking to break your mind or wreck your religion, but isn't that equating you to sheep? Yeah, religions use that metaphor a lot.

Question:
- Are you seeing the light yet?

Action:
- Keep reading.

>>><<<

Beyond Our Ability

I suspect some of you are stuck in the religious aspects of life. If so, you may be about to close your mind to what I'm saying here. Just for your sake, I'm going to use the Bible as my example, a part of it which, I believe, few people have really considered in depth.

The Bible talks about the "omnipotence" of God—everywhere, everywhen, within everything—all-knowing. I believe that is so. Again, as everything is energy in some form or other, wouldn't that be like saying God is all of it—all the particles of energy and/or all that is between?

In the humble essence of this, our world, *it doesn't fucking matter.*

But the truth, however you choose to see it, is that God is infinite. And being as we, here on this planet, only know the duality of things—that everything in this plane has a *from* and a *to*, a beginning and an end—we don't really know a thing until we know and have some inkling of its breadth. There's sweet to sour, hot to cold, and even, in our judgmental minds, there is right to wrong. Get it?

We have no experience of infinity. We are incapable of understanding it beyond its simple definition. And God, the Higher Power, is infinite—no beginning, no end.

Despite everything your religions are telling you, do you think we even have the ability to "know" the full extent of that Higher Power beyond the slightest touch of God's energy shared with our higher soul part out beyond our consciousness?

So, at this point, I'm going to leave you gasping at the ramifications of this law with this simple statement of fact: We—physically, mentally, and spiritually—are a part of this Universe.

Questions:

- Yeah, I'm repeating the concept AGAIN. And yeah, this is a little different take than your religions offer. Is it getting any clearer for you?
- What do we know about that Higher Power—God?
- Or maybe the real question is, what are we capable of knowing about an infinite being?
- What do we know about man? Given that God is an infinite source of power, we know there is no question that man, in his greed, will abuse that power . . . given the chance.
- And of ourselves? Through our belief in God, why would we give him that chance?
- Are you offended? Or bored?
- Do you think religion is using the Bible just to keep us separated, to keep us needing religion to get in touch with God?

- Do you think that is because the Bible was written by a lot of different people, each having their own opinions and purposes . . . and greed?
- Was it written by man but inspired by God? I'm not saying it wasn't. But being the actual WORD OF GOD? Do you think it is? Or is it that organized religions demand that you believe, just for the sake of their own control over you? What else is there for religion to control, BUT YOU?
- Me? I question religion's motives—but God's? I look to the love. ***Control is NEVER love.***

Actions:

- ➤ Again, I'm not trying to wreck your faith in God. I am—AGAIN—asking you to do your own FUCKING thinking.
- ➤ Your name is not B-b-braaad-ley or B-b-beeet-ty, or is it? Take a moment. Once you have settled down to an even simmer, write about it.

It's Homophoric

Saying something that supports someone who you know is lying to themselves—saying it just because you know it will bolster up their ego—is that a gift?

Oh, they will absolutely like you for it, but being liked is about you. Being of service? That's about them.

Ah, but in this world where so many lies abound, all of which just allow you to live those lies in relative comfort—"relative" in that your comfort ignores the painful consequences—when the truth comes around, those consequences always suck.

Saying the truth up front may not win you any friends. Those, in the end, who will look at the truth will appreciate you—

REALLY appreciate you—but they will always be the few. No one wants to see themselves as being "WRONG."

But then, what if "right and wrong" were only the shit from between someone's ears? When put on a serving plate, it is only the gilding on that plate that makes what is on it look so desirable. What if that gilding, that shiny, gold covering, is the belief that they are the "authority" but you are not?

So, the truth is really about a journey that only you can take, a lonely search wherein you will find few accompanying you. There are so few in this life who will do their own thinking and admit when that thinking is ever fucked up. It's not about being "right or wrong."

And "truth"—those things about life that, like gravity, always hold true? What if that was always right there in plain sight? There, where only those willing to let go of "right and wrong" can see it?

It has been there, just so, you know. Like the law of gravity, it is only a law because it "just is." These laws of truth are most often called "Spiritual Laws." Spiritual, only because life itself is all a spiritual experience. It is only because the word "spiritual" gets all tangled up in some kind of homophoric viewpoint where it is sexually associated with those passionately "religious."

"Homophoric?" You question if that is even a word? IT ISN'T. It is no more a real word than there is any real relationship between being "spiritual" and being "religious." Think about that one.

Questions:
- Am I being too esoteric?
- Or maybe too redneck?
- The subject matter is pretty deep. It's a conundrum— yeah, it still sometimes puzzles me. What about you?

- I call the Spiritual Laws "the simple truths" of life. In this book, maybe they aren't so simple. They—every one—can get deep. I try to keep it in your face and straight to the point. Am I just shitting myself? Is it truly the stuff from plumbing the depths in Rumi's outhouse?

Action:

➢ Is there anything, so far, wherein you think I'm shitting you? Write about it.

>>><<<

It's About the Energy

It's all about the energy. There's love and there's everything that is not love (fear).

I considered writing a book covering the more negative side—the Liberal side—of life. Their philosophy is just the opposite of my own. New Thought makes it clear that you do have a choice in the energy with which you run your life. Unlike Liberals, we most generally choose love.

I thought I'd title such a book, *Frankly, My Dear, I DON'T GIVE A SHIT!* The problem with that sentiment is that it is the choice of no energy or feelings. It is being dead to life. Someone who doesn't give a shit is abdicating all their feelings, their passion. The best they can expect in life is constipation. And the end? That's gotta be a shitstorm.

In my rush to get my first ten books published, I neglected to promote them. So, I'm not that well known. Now I'm wondering . . . what with there being so much negativity in the world today, validating the negative side, is that what people want from me? That's not what I want.

So how do I deal with the woke side—those victim-minded folks who take offense every chance they get, who prefer to live in an energy of negativity? What to do. So far in this series, I have made it a point to warn them not to read. As an author, I don't need negative reviews. Even so, I can appreciate them for telling me who they are. Maybe it's about my own energy. How loving have I been? Am I stretching the energy of LOVE by mixing it with TRUTH?

Can I offer anyone a better choice without being an example in my own life? No. I must hold them capable of running their own life. Who am I to decide what you, the reader, will accept? Maybe you are the exact person who will need and appreciate what I have to say—even appreciate it being punctuated with a few curse words. So, read on.

This book might offer you the ultimate in pissed off. Or possibly the knowledge that there is a better choice. Hopefully, whatever it offers, you will take it with all your passion and run with it—or from it. Either way, you will be going somewhere in life . . . somewhere far away from "don't give a shit."

Here is a sample thought from that side:
Yup, you've got me pegged. I'm one of those redneck conservatives who doesn't care if you want to take offense. You see, I'm not a victim in my life. If you are in yours, I'd appreciate it if you keep your feelings to yourself. Liberals generally make piss-poor choices in the "feelings" department, and I just don't want to be close enough to get sprayed.

Your feelings are TOTALLY your own. When you take offense with ANYTHING, you make yourself a victim to that thing. I don't want a thing to do with your "thing"—if that means making yourself my victim—not when I'm doing my own personal thing that gives joy to my life.

What you don't seem to "get" is that other people don't give a rat's ass about you or your feelings, not if you are a megalomaniac asshole. That kind of friend just naturally gets a fella sprayed. Having your back would only ensure that of being a *really . . . super . . . bad . . . experience.*

Oh, and BTW, I can understand why you'd think there is a shortage of toilet paper, which brings us back to that law talked about from the beginning of this book and repeated ad nauseam. Yeah . . . it takes a lot of toilet paper to keep that shit wiped up.

Remember that truth about life saying that there are only two types of energy to choose from in the living of life? *There is love, and there is everything that is not love (fear).*

Again, "don't give a shit" is on the opposite side of the love energy. It is also on the opposite side of the fear energy. It is the state of "no energy." It takes you completely out of this box of rocks we call Earth.

If you don't have it in you to be loving—and you don't understand which of the various forms of fear you would replace it with and why—then perhaps "don't give a shit" just gives you a little breathing space. Certainly, in that space, you aren't making that critical choice in the energy in which you are living.

HOWEVER, abdicating your responsibility in this life is not something your soul will tolerate for long, and your soul has your reset button, y'know?

Questions:
- There are some things we care about more than others. Are there some things you don't give a shit about?
- How about people? Are there any you don't give a shit about?
- Is that about a lack of interest or a lack of caring?

- So, okay, let's just split that pubic hair. If your answer is "lack of caring," you gotta know that it is the opposite of love AND it is also the opposite of fear as well. If the definition of "don't give a shit" is to abdicate living, how long do you think your soul will put up with you being in this life?

Action:
- ➢ Keep your pubes intact. And don't piss off your soul. Find it within yourself to choose to love others.

PART FIVE
Relationships

Remember how you don't truly know a thing until you have experienced the full gamut—from the ecstasy to the shittery? There is no better way to gain that experience than in a relationship.

Real Love

Y'know, love isn't the purpose of relationships. It is only the frosting on the cake. The cake—the real purpose—is the meeting of needs.

Your soul is that highest part of who you are. As a being of energy, that part is closest, in fact, IS the energy of God. Those needs are, in reality, your soul's—GOD'S—need to experience life. To experience a thing takes knowing that part of life from the ecstasy to the shittery, the full gamut.

But love? REAL LOVE? Once given, it can never be taken back. Real love is eternal. When one's needs change or are no longer being met, then is when a relationship is over. For life to be functional, one must then move on. *Yet the love goes on forever.*

And BTW, ladies . . . what you say about your ex, the energy you put out, tells all us guys if you are a loving woman—or not. Loving someone is never something you will ever regret.

Yeah, I know. I sound like a fucking preacher. My bad! It's so hard to love someone who just wants to control you. That goes double for relationships.

And yes, in letting my first wife carry my balls in her pocket, that begs the question: Was my love REAL love—or just REAL fear?

Thing is, in REAL life, we all vacillate between the two energies: love or fear. When looking back, one can see in which energy one generally was choosing to live. But that clarity only comes because one no longer has control of "what was." What's in one's face now is "what is."

And what is? Do you love them still? Or did you just want to love them back then, but failed?

Questions:
- Love is a gift, and gifts carry no expectations, no stipulations—no expiration, y'know?
- Can you see that if you are carrying harsh feelings after parting, then the truth of your love is that you never loved them at all?
- There are only the two energies: LOVE and everything that is not love (FEAR). Anger, vindictiveness, disappointment, sadness, hurt . . . do you get that these are NOT the energy of love?

Action:
- ➢ It is pretty much a certainty that you've had at least one failed relationship. Examine how you felt about that person when it ended. Answer honestly. Did you wish them the very best in their lives afterward? Do your feelings, right now, tell you that you truly loved them then—or not? Either way, it is okay. Life is about the lessons, about your growth, about becoming more than you were.

>>><<<

The Thing About Love

The thing about love is that if you don't have any for yourself, then you have none to give to another. So who gives you the love you have for yourself?

YOU DO.

How can you when it is not there? Ah, that's the kicker. It is only our fear that makes it so. You see, YOU need to look inside yourself—something everyone is afraid to do because of what we think we will see. Thing is, if you will have the courage to look—loving courage—you will discover the truth.

SO, WHAT IS THE TRUTH?

Truth is, we are as a drop in the sea of God. WE ARE GOD—a part of Him/Her/It. To catch just one glimpse of that FACT will fill you with such magnificence that you will fall in love. It is that soul part which is consciously God that gives that to you.

Your life here is about the lessons your soul gives you to learn. The answers are all inside, waiting for you to discover them for yourself. The fact you are reading this book tells me clearly: Your soul is telling you to take that inner journey and this book is but one step along your way.

Questions:
- One Of the best ways of making such a connection with your soul is through meditation? Have you meditated?
- If so, did you ever make that connection to the magnificence?

Actions:
- ➢ Learn to meditate and write about it.
- ➢ Keep a record of all such experiences.

Taking It Personal

Folks, to a reader, a story is not always "just a story." Stories taken from real life have much more impact. The following is from my own personal life. If you want more, it is all laid out in detail in my book, *The Courage of a Butterfly*, and in its sequel, *The Soul of an Eagle.*

Even before meeting the Specter of Death in that ICU, my perception of love was different from the norm. Was it something ingrained in me by my soul in a different incarnation? It seems I was following the Spiritual Laws concerning love even before I learned them. I'm going to share my experience with you.

On a soul level, you do feel another person's love. It is a very uplifting thing, but for most, it is an unconscious thing. On a conscious level of mind—the level in this life—you can only feel your love for them. Want to know how I know this?
PERSONAL EXPERIENCE.

I was married for over twenty-six years to a woman whom I loved dearly. REAL love, not the fake, egotistical control that so many call love. What makes me so sure my love was real— how do I know? It's because there was nothing that she could do to change that in me. There was no wrong that she could do, and few that she didn't, that could make me stop loving her.

My love for her will last until I die, and then some. The ONLY reason I divorced her was because the relationship no longer worked, nor could I make it work. It takes two.

Relationships are about the meeting of one another's needs. To love someone is only one of those needs. To be loved, cherished, and respected are others. I had none of that and so I told myself lies.

You see, she was the love of my life. I was her security, and not much else, and I was not willing to consciously acknowledge it. Given even a little self-respect, that truth would have required my whole life to change—and to change without her. I knew it but would not consciously admit it.

Then a minor accident while ski-tubing in Lake Powell caused a blood clot in my leg. A week later found me in an ICU with a massive clot between my lungs and heart—the kind most folks don't survive.

The doctors didn't expect me to live. Hell, I didn't expect me to live. The ONLY reason I did, I believe, was because I got honest about it all. My soul may have hit the reset button, but I wasn't ready to go.

Point is, that while the marriage resulted in failure, I didn't stop loving her. That love was a rare gift I gave myself because I felt every minute of it—a love that few ever get to experience.

**AND I DON'T REGRET HAVING LOVED HER
ALL THAT TIME.**

It is NOT about the OTHER person's love for you. It IS about your love for THEM. This is your life, no one else's, and you can't MAKE another person feel something they don't want to feel. But you CAN feel what YOU want to feel.

Now, I've just given you the lead story into my memoir books—both of them. If you want to know anything more, you'll just have to buy them. I guarantee these books, either one, will not be what you expect. Few people are set up to know the things these books will tell you.

Questions:
- Were you ever in a relationship where you loved them, but were not loved back?
- Did you stay? Did you too, lie to yourself—stay stuck in your drama? Real love is eternal. If you can't love them forever and yet simply move on in your life, then it was never your love, rather your fear.
- And in lying to yourself? Do you realize, that is you, being disloyal to your soul—the one who has your reset button?

Actions:
- ➤ I won't try to tell you to "fess-up." We both know the price you will pay. I will tell you that it is a price worth paying. The Universe always balances.
- ➤ Don't let it become a matter of living or dying like I did.

Practice What I Preach

Y'know, men like to make love with their women, then as they roll over and . . . well, just before the snoring takes place, the thought likely is, *Yeah . . . really nailed her good!* But what is going through *her* mind? Likely, it is frustration.

Is it any wonder that a woman might cheat? Or maybe she just turns to bisexuality. Most men see that as titillating, in a kinky sort of way. After all, he doesn't feel threatened by what tastes good to her. Likely, it is not the taste she likes, but rather, it is being tasted. And then there is being cared about.

I've always thought of myself as above all that "usual guy bullshit." I mean, I always did my best to make it satisfying for the woman. But did I?

My first wife only orgasmed once in the over twenty-five years of our marriage. That one time left a lot of doubt in my mind. Did she want strange man meat? Was I not doing enough in the beginning to prepare her for sex?

While my equipment was considered only slightly larger than the normal six inches, maybe I still wasn't big enough.

What . . . WHAT?

Later, after the divorce, I heard no complaints. And while I only took women on one at a time sexually, except for all the drama and discord it would have caused, I could have taken on more. But then, very few women will put up with a "player." Besides, "more" was never what I wanted, and cheating would have required a lot of dishonesty. That just wasn't okay with me.

Ah, yes, sexuality really runs the gamut. Straight, bi, gay— how much of it is done in the darkness with cheating? I've never been a jealous man, never felt a need to check my woman's panties for unwanted stains.

So, I don't know. Maybe I just gave them all respect by believing they were being honest with me. How much love can a relationship have if YOU fill it with such fearful shit?

Nowadays, things have changed, and I've been forced to look deeper at the lesbian side of it all. Being lesbian doesn't make them not human. They, too, are susceptible to the fearful shit, like cheating.

But then, a lot of people, given the choice, would rather be dishonest. Some find that exciting. But for the most part, it seems to me that lesbians generally are much better satisfied than are straight women. But what would I know? I've never been a lesbian—until now.

I do know that they are experts in the tasty side of sex and seem to thoroughly enjoy the whole range of sex toys. Takes real expertise to correlate all that successfully. That, and the emotional needs, all boil down to caring and great, long-term foreplay. That is the way of it, or so it seems to me.

Me? I've been a diabetic for many years now. As it always does, diabetes eventually ruins a guy's sexual ability. But no one talks about that, do they?

For me, it appeared there was no choice but to give up sex altogether. I'd lost it in the man-meat department, but still had it going, upstairs, within the gray matter department. I've always had it going in the caring department.

In fact, the caring is where it is at for me now. There is nothing I find more sexually satisfying than being worshiped by a well-satisfied woman, as in—

"Oh God . . . oh God . . . oh g-a--a-a-ah . . . Gawddddd!"

Sure, when meeting a woman, I could keep my mouth shut—until that moment of truth when they either run raging into the night or submit to what I offer. Some might then get past the clog between their ears and enjoy it.

But for me, this is not an option. It is a lie of omission—dishonest. But to put the truth of my situation out there in this society? Not a good idea. No matter. I really don't give a shit what others think of me. And still, I'm not you. There are those who get their self-esteem by demeaning others among themselves.

Lesbian women, in general . . . well, let's face it, many just hate men. And straight women are fixated on man meat, and, of course, the lube job in whichever end. So, I have had very few sexual relationships over the last several years, and they always end because of me.

You see, just as "normal" sexual relationships are often dissatisfying for a woman, most "normal" love relationships are generally dissatisfying for me. When a person has that "normal victim-thinking mentality," what always goes with it is a need to control those with whom they are close.

That control always comes from the energy of fear. In the end, the relationship seldom consists of much love. I'm looking for a woman who can understand me and doesn't feel that victim need to control.

Yeah, I think differently. I don't want a love relationship where control—complete with all of its accompanying drama—has replaced the love. I don't want a "normal" relationship.

Heart-on-the-sleeve shit? It's usually a turnoff. My sexuality-on-my-sleeve stance may be the same. At this point, I'm sure that what is going through your mind may be shortened to TMI—too much information.

But like a good redneck, I'm going there anyway. Thing is, *if you are afraid of what others might think of you, then you can never be authentic.* It's time to practice what I preach.

Preach—PREACH? Oh . . . my . . . God!

After all the personal disgust I've expressed about organized religion and its preachers, here I am acknowledging myself as a preacher. Is it even possible to preach at people without it being a demand that they live the same beliefs as I have concerning that Higher Power—God?

Yeah, I talk a lot about "God" only because, in my mind, it's so much easier than saying Higher Power. It is not meant as being a "religious" thing, but rather "spiritual." There is a big difference.

What is my expectation here? Do I expect anyone to see life the same way I do? Hope . . . maybe. Expect . . . no. I offer you my honesty, fully realizing that "honesty" is not the way this society has ever taught us to be—especially when a man is discussing his sexuality.

Nor do I have expectations of anything beyond ridicule. And I certainly don't expect the ladies to line up for the "good ol' boy lesbian sex experience." No, the best I can expect is that some folks reading this might display some honesty in their own lives. Honesty, because I wrote these words in perfect alignment with who I am.

The only real and true expectation I can, and do, have is with my own honesty. Perhaps that is just the first step out of the box that humanity, and its preachers, would have us all live within—a box I just don't want to be in anymore.

There is a shitload of guys in my same situation. Likely, a lot of them would rather be alone and lonely than to be honest.

But what about you women? Does your man float in this boat? Do you miss sexual gratification and suave his conscience by saying you don't?

I've offered my own take on it here. Have you discussed this with him? If his own gratification ever went past himself, he likely now has a chance to discover the true gift in sexual giving.

That his situation sucks down on his ego—his sense of self—is a guarantee. What would it mean to him, to you both, should you find yourself honestly screaming out in ecstasy? I know what it means to me.

Questions:
- Are you living alone without a partner?
- Is it because you don't want to have to be honest with them about your situation? Are you afraid of the consequences of telling the truth?
- Is it that you don't like sex? Or maybe you like it too much and are afraid he or she will find out just how kinky you really are?
- Do you get out that toy to give yourself meager satisfaction in the dark of night? Wouldn't it be more satisfying to have another human being to run that vibrating doohickey for you—with pleasure?
- Why? Why choose to be alone?

Action:
- ➤ Have the courage—courage to get naked—to face the ridicule and be honest. You will find that there is a shitload of partners out there with your same fears . . . a significant other who will admire you and appreciate the honesty you are showing because it has set them free to step past their own fear.

Addiction

I'm gonna change gears here and make this one about ADDICTION. That's not to say I've ever had an addiction to any of those things that turn most people's lives into major misery: drugs, alcohol, etc. And no, I'm no expert on other people's addictions — only my own.

Yes, I have had my own addictions plaguing my life. And the cure? I suspect there is no cure. Mine has come back to plague me several times over, and I've been stopped each time. It seems to have one common thread: MY EGO.

The ego is nothing more than the sense of self. The word carries a stench ONLY in that one does not speak about it in a positive sense, whereas that positive sense is its main purpose for being. Let me explain.

When I was younger, I tried drugs in a minor way — Mary Jane and hash. The reason I never went further down that trail was that I didn't like the way my mind responded. Sure, there was a certain euphoria, a sense that the world is okay and everything is cool . . . mostly.

But for me, I didn't like that my perception of it all, my sense of self, was constantly changing uncontrollably. Yeah, that uncontrollable part — that "I'm no longer in charge of my thinking" part — is why I never became a drug addict, in that I bailed out on Mary Jane and never went after the things that were harder.

I suppose, even then, I had some sense of the Spiritual Laws, particularly the one that states: *Everything begins with a thought.* Bottom line, this law is the key to ending all addiction. You simply gotta NOT want it to a much greater extent than you DO want it.

My addiction was smoking. I started as an eight-year-old lifting smokes from the one general store in the uranium mining camp of Fry Canyon, Utah. Yeah, the pretense of this adult thing called cigarettes was attractive.

I didn't actually begin breathing it in until later, as a teenager in Greece. Wanting to be as cool as the others at the American Academy in Athens. But the fact was, it was just NOT cool, but it was where the real habit began.

Thing was, my brother, Mike, and I were not the children of military high brass or government officials. We were nobodies—low-echelon bosses' kids whose dads were there working on a diversion tunnel for a dam on the Achelous River. We were NOT cool. Once free of that snobbish academy and out roaming the Greek countryside, we smoked freely because, by then, we enjoyed it.

The first time I actually quit was at the grand old age of thirty. I awoke one morning, sitting there on the edge of my bed, hacking and coughing. I began to realize how really shitty smoking was making my body feel. I quit, cold turkey, and didn't start again until the drama in my marriage, and the resulting divorce, drove me to replace the pain created by her loss. That called for an addiction that held more pleasant memories—smoking. And yes, I was also addicted to my wife, despite all her dramas.

Are you getting a sense of my victimhood yet? Yeah, my first wife was my addiction. Or rather, the fact that I loved her, really loved her . . . so much so, that I couldn't perceive living my life without her.

My only problem was that about once a month, I'd piss her off in some minor way and she'd demand a divorce. I'd beg, tell her anything, swear to change my whole life to suit hers.

'Course, everyone gets to be who they are. Me, too. Can't change that unless I want to. I didn't, so despite honest intentions, it was only a pretense. She'd slip my balls back into her own pocket for the next month, then take them out, once again, for the squeezing.

And then there is that one Spiritual Law—again. It states that *there are only two energies in which we are living our lives: LOVE and everything that is NOT love (fear)*. It's an either/or thing. The two energies cannot coincide.

For the most part, I loved her. It was only during those times when she felt her control slipping that I turned to fear. Then it was that I became that whining, crying pussy who believed he couldn't live without her.

That was when I found myself in that ICU and the immediate, unquestionable presence of my death. I could no longer tell myself that lie. I survived but put my balls back in my own pocket. For the next eighteen months, I tried to control and change her—everyone has their learning curve. It didn't work for me any better than it had for her.

Eventually, she slipped and made her old, trusty demand for a divorce once again, and I could no longer lie to myself or pretend for her.

In my perception, my ego—my sense of self—came to realize that I COULD live my life without her. I COULD, and I COULD still love her. It no longer required that we be together in that sick, fucking, dysfunctional relationship that she demanded it be—the one I no longer accepted.

With a pain-filled heart, I set her free.

It is from personal experience that I can tell you that ALL addictions demand that you be someone you don't want to be. When you perceive the unacceptable truth of it . . . when you "get" how disloyal that is to your soul . . . you can, and will, stop the addiction.

Everything does begin with a thought, and sometimes, ends with one, too. Often, it is just a matter of whose pocket those cajoles are in.

Oh, and there is still that one other thing: I was, and still am, addicted to female companionship with all its benefits. That's not to say that I ever cheated on any of the women with whom I've been involved sexually. I haven't.

But with my second wife, I thought we had a perfect relationship. There was just one thing I needed that she wouldn't provide. And yes, I did consider getting that need met elsewhere, but it had to be honest and consensual. We considered swinging. Didn't happen, probably because neither of us wanted it to.

In the end, it was she who kicked me to the curb—rightfully so. The only way I could have avoided it was to force her to look at something she didn't want to see. That was something I wouldn't do. I looked at myself and dealt with my own shit about it. She got to be herself with me. In the end, it was the fact that I ever had an issue that made me unacceptable to her.

'Nuff said! If you want the full story, you'll have to read the sequel book, *The Soul of an Eagle*. I had a problem dealing with being honest about this one issue in particular when writing it—in fact, it held up publication for several years.

For me now? Yes, there's still that need for companionship. But as for sex, things change. For me to have safe sex now requires more than just a single, rubber glove—or a woman who can understand my philosophy.

I've written that part of the story into two of the books in this *Redneck Spirituality* series. Besides, being addicted to always having a woman with benefits is covered en masse in my sequel novel, *The Soul of an Eagle*. It is no longer a need, but simply a want.

As for God? He/She/It seems so bent on creating life, I have to consider that maybe that Higher Power is addicted to companionship, too. And companionship? I don't see that as an addiction. When you love yourself, it just naturally follows that you will spread your love to others. Perhaps truth is, we all need companionship. Isn't that a growth requirement— loving someone besides ourselves?

Questions:
- Do you see companionship as a need?
- Is the "with benefits" part a need or a want?
- For you, is it something to be sought after? Or is it required?
- Or if you already have a companion, do you nurture him or her?
- Do you always accept sex when it is offered? By your partner? By others? Together with others?

Actions:
- Face it, we are social animals. We need companionship. Before you start a sexual relationship, get honest with one another. Tell them exactly what your needs are. Tell them about any sexual kinks you have—about your every embarrassing fantasies. You don't want to find yourself getting any needs met dishonestly behind one another's back. Those kinky, little fantasies may actually be your soul's needs. We are not always consciously aware of those soul needs, but with your soul, its needs are demands.
- Whatever you do, do it with **honesty**. If you're the guy, would your relationship survive having your significant other catch you, balls-deep, in someone else's ass? Likely, the only way it might is if you both have the same kink and both are honest about it.

All the Lonely People . . .

I'm clear that when you're alone in your world, the only thing you can take comfort against that loneliness is by sincerely enjoying your own company. Yeah, takes a little growing, but I've accomplished that—MOST OF THE TIME. Those times when I don't, I gotta admit, it's because I sometimes slip into my past, the "if only" of relationships done.

Maybe it would be different for me if I hadn't had so many really GREAT relationships, all of whom I loved. Did they all love me back? Dunno. That is none of my business. What was—and maybe will be again—is that I loved them to the very best of my capability. For a time, we gave one another what we needed in life.

Problem is, our needs are always transitory. Change is the constant of the Universe. When a person's needs have been met, or are being met, they grow past them. Their new needs were sometimes something I could not meet.

We parted, and I'm proud to say it was NEVER with hard feelings on my part. I can't say it was always so for them. AGAIN, that was none of my business.

What was would be how I dealt with my own shit.

There were few releases from the bowels of my own mind wherein I didn't have a smooth movement. Parting often comes with a little pain as your shit exits the sphincter of your mind. It only hurts when that asshole doesn't want to stretch—and to accept. Such stretching is not about the pain. It is about the growing, learning to be loving, especially with yourself. That is a normal, natural process and part of the human experience.

Seems like most of the ladies my age prefer to be alone. Is that because they've grown to like their own company in a pleasant present, or because they are stuck reliving the pain of past, unhappy relationships?

AND, it is STILL none of my business. But you gotta know that it doesn't take long to read their energy and know if I want them in my life. Ladies with a pleasant "present" are a delightful discovery for me.

Do I NEED them? No. I just WANT to travel through my life in the company of a loving woman.

Wants and needs are not the same thing. Needs are a thing of the NEEDY, akin to just being a human with an unfulfilled soul. Wants are about reaching for your joy.

Do they need me? You've GOT it . . . that's also none of my fucking business. Well, okay. The "fucking" part is just about joy for those who find joy that way.

Questions:
- Oooooh wheee! Is that judgment squirting out of the sphincter of your mind?
- Yes, we rednecks are what most judge as being rude, yet the subject here is reality. Shit, in all its forms, is something we ALL do—both from the bowels of our minds and those of our ass. My question here is: How do you do it? With or without judgment?
- Do you know that with judgment, it is YOU wiping YOURS on them?

Action:
- ➤ Become aware—very aware—of your own judgments.

The Truth of the Lie

Y'know, a lot of marriages end when one partner cheats. The fucking part is not the issue. The issue is honesty and trust. With wife number two, neither one of us cheated. But in the end, I wasn't the person she accepted. What was it she saw wrong in me? I dunno.

Was it a question of my loyalty or her own disloyalty? Clearly, she no longer believed in me. Whatever she saw in her mind about me, she judged as wrong. Truth was, I loved her and would still be there, but that was no longer my choice.

It is so much easier to blame others for what one won't even look at concerning one's self. And yet, it WAS in my life and I DID create it. The blame for that is not on her. How could it be? Blame is always a lie.

I loved her, but if you want to be with someone, it is required that they be acceptable in your mind. Initially, that was a struggle for me, but I won my struggle and accepted her without demanding she change. That is what acceptance is all about.

Eight years into our relationship, she discovered that truth— my truth as she saw it—about that struggle. The fact that there ever was a struggle to accept her made me now unacceptable. Go figure.

With a broken heart, I released her with love. That is the truth about that book, this book, and my life. The marriage vows written herein are indeed the ones we took. Those vows are summed up in the last two stanzas:

In the eternity of time

should we part,
your heart from mine,
our parting will be as our starting . . .
in honesty and truth and love.

(Repeated by the other . . .)
(Then repeated together . . .)

In honesty and truth and love,
You are free to be YOU, with ME.

I am alone now, and I wonder if there is a woman out there who values truth and has the courage to take responsibility for everything in her life rather than to blame.

Ah, but doesn't our Christian religion give God credit for all the good shit in our lives, hold Satan responsible for all the evil we do, and allow us to blame our significant others when we are not happy? We have all been taught that we are never the responsible party for anything involving our feelings.

Me? I can honestly say I loved every one of the ladies mentioned in that last novel, *The Soul of an Eagle.* Beyond that, I can also say that I never tried to change any of them. That is what it looks like to unconditionally accept someone. Real love is unconditional. When someone is trying to change you, that is how you know you are not being accepted. In that novel, that is what happened to me, from every woman.

Ah, but it appears our society has taught us so many lies, the worst of which, it seems, bites most every man on the ass. Women want security, and in that endeavor, they need control.

But there is no security in life. And control? The other person has to give that to you and, without fail, will eventually take it away.

There's that Spiritual Law, *I am the Creator*, and for a man who lives that law, there cannot even be a pretense of being controlled or controlling.

Giving control away is a sham, a façade, that every insecure woman shoots for in a man, only to find that it will kill her relationship—EVERY TIME—once the target is acquired.

The law is the law. No one will allow someone else to run their life forever. Dreading the penalty that he will pay in stepping out of line is what keeps him there. Yes, it's comfortable standing in line there behind that boss hog, but eventually, she will need to shit.

Now I know how salmon feel in swimming upstream just to spawn—arduous and always in danger from the jaws of the bear. The bear got me in both my marriages. That's a tough one to deal with when you're just swimming upstream, wanting to spawn.

And spawning? It is such a wondrous thing. It's more than just the fucking. It's about the companionship. It's about having someone who believes in you, and you have each other's back, no matter what. But most of all, it is about having an opportunity to love someone.

Again, the nitty-gritty physicality about love is that you actually can only feel the energy of your own love for another. You cannot feel the energy they are feeling, outside of the things they do when being nice to you.

But those things will end when your payment check bounces. It takes the energy of love from both parties to make a relationship work. REAL love, where neither party demands a payment. Unfortunately, one partner's demand for control is often mistaken for real love. It is seldom seen for what it actually is—a payment.

"If you love me, you'll live your life to suit mine."

This is the bottom-line truth of the lie that then passes for their love. When one partner lives that lie while calling it love, it takes a strong love for the other to stay. Can a relationship stand were that lie to be so from both? Not a fucking chance.

Questions:
- Has the energy of your "love" ever been controlling? Playing the game of control is what we—whether as a swinging dick or bouncing ta-tas—have all been taught to do. Most then see that as love.
- And that control? Do you realize that is only about changing them to be who we want them to be?
- Do you realize that if they try to be that, it is only a pretense, a lie? It is NOT love.
- This is the game most everyone plays together and calls it a relationship—a "loving" relationship. Have you ever played that game?
- Are you seeing how badly the lies of society are fucking up everyone's life?
- Do you realize that the lessons our souls are here to give you are always about the truths—the ones these Spiritual Laws are all about?
- Could it be that your soul is what put this book in your hands just now?

Action:
- ➢ Find what you need to do, and do it.

God Gives You All the Good Shit

Does God really give us all the good shit in life? YES! But that statement doesn't include our own part in it all. If, as the Bible states, God is within us all, then doesn't the reverse speak the truth as well? WE ARE WITHIN GOD. WE ARE PART OF GOD—the part that gives God the experience of this life

As such, we have access to the power. It is through our access and use of it that we create attracting everything we want in life. YOUR life is about YOU. That is, YOU, this little piece of God.

Our ability to create the "good shit" is done through the grace in our connection with God, not BY God's grace.

Oh, but to acknowledge that would be to take the power of God out of the hands of religion. But wouldn't that mean that WE don't need religion to be in contact with God?

As for our unhappiness being the fault of our significant other? NO, it's our OWN fault. The joy we experience in being in a relationship is wrapped up totally in our love for them. We are the ones who actually feel our love. Our happiness or unhappiness is a personal choice. So, too, it is the same with feeling our love.

Sure, there is a spiritual energy, an upliftment, in being loved back. But that is felt at the upper level beyond our consciousness—the soul-to-soul level.

Questions:
- Do you get that pretty much everyone in this world is in a continued struggle to control other people?
- That, in part, is why we try to demand their love.
- Is control ever love?

- Can your joy ever be any better than it is when giving the gift of love to yourself and others?

Actions:

➢ Live your life in the energy of love.

➢ Take fucking responsibility for your life. NO one—not even your significant other—wants to take the blame for your inability to love.

➢ Do you think an almighty God needs, or wants, credit for your ability to create ANYTHING in your life that you think of as "good shit?"

>>><<<

Reba's Song

This one was prompted by Reba's song, "Just Like Them Horses." It begins with the words, "How do you say goodbye?"

It all started when I divorced my first wife. I didn't know it, but she'd been in touch with my parents, telling them about how I was losing my sanity all during the eighteen months it took me to accept the fact that I was simply her security in a life where there is no such thing.

I was never the love of her life. Yeah, for twenty-five years, I lied to myself that she saw me that way. It took the presence of the Angel of Death in that ICU to show me the sad truth of my life.

The struggle then was all mine. In her mind, I was fucked up—but she was okay. She never looked at the truth. But then, she never experienced the Angel with his fist inside her chest, squeezing the life out of her while demanding honesty for life to continue. That was my struggle, and I kept it to myself until the decision was made.

Since her rants demanding a divorce no longer worked, she suffered on in silence—to me—but not to my parents. Ironically, my decision was made when, after about eighteen months, she slipped and demanded another divorce. I gave it to her, accepting that who she was just didn't work in my life. I called my parents to tell them the sad news.

Can't say I wasn't hoping—no, expecting—their support for me then in this, the darkest moment of my life. Instead, I got their own rant about what a slimy slug they saw me as being, one not even fit to inhabit the lowest level in the family outhouse. Unless I stayed married and fulfilled my "obligations" as a husband, I was no longer welcome in their home.

That was the way it remained for the next fifteen years until their deaths. It didn't matter what I said or did, I was that slimy slug. And I was NEVER able to say goodbye, and oh . . . how I tried.

Play Reba's song, "Just Like Them Horses." Listen to the heartbreak in that one-liner, "How do you say goodbye?" That line cut me to the soul.

Questions:
- Y'know, when a Catholic son doesn't live his life the way his parents demand, the threat he faces is to be burned in hell. Mormons believe in three degrees of Heaven— THERE IS NO MORMON HELL. Can you guess what a son or daughter is then threatened with?
  Excommunication? I didn't give a rat's ass about that.
- No, I was disowned by all the family I had, unacceptable to everyone I loved. How do I phrase that into a question? Only one way works: *How fucked up is that?*

Action:
- If you have ever had a similar experience, write about it.

>>><<<

Somewhere Out There . . .

As mentioned, I've written two novels. Both start out in an ICU, and both have a fictional character named Big D, the Angel of Death. In that first book—*The Courage of a Butterfly*—I tell the Angel the story of my past. With every chapter, he shows me what it looks like in the light of the Spiritual Laws. Seeing it illuminated by those simple truths gives a very different perspective, one from which very few ever get to look.

The sequel—*The Soul of an Eagle*—then travels forward. It tells about how I came to discover those truths. It is the story of my journey along "The Road Less Travelled," a time of great discovery for me. At the same time, it was an exercise in frustration where the women in my life then were concerned.

There was the divorce from the love of my life. I didn't quit loving her, but me being this "out of her control person" no longer worked in our lives together.

Several more women then danced through my life—women who also had no clue about what love is. I loved every one of them, but bottom line, consciously or unconsciously, each thought loving someone was an exercise in control. That IS what our society teaches us all. I was no longer playing that game.

Then came a very special woman, one who *did* understand the game and also didn't play. But relationships are about personal growth. They provide us with the very best lessons we will ever have in life. Most will have many lessons, but all will have something—some little, earthshaking thing—one has to deal with about one's self that will rattle your very life. Mine certainly did.

I dealt with my shit, I thought, and was happily living the life I believed we both wanted. That shit wasn't something I kept from her in the beginning, just something she didn't think she needed to change about herself. And as I was *not* about changing her to suit me, that left me with changing me. Ah, but a relationship is about both parties, and most lessons involve both. What that lesson was about for me was easy. For her it was not.

The years flew by—eight of them—and I was drawing that sequel book to a close with her and me riding off into the sunset. Ah, but that was not to be. A snake wriggled herself back into our lives and put the fact that I ever had an issue into my wife's face, a fact that was about her part of the lesson. In dealing with my part, it seemed that for my wife, her part was left hanging— an equally stupid, little thing that now she would not get past.

I knew there was nothing I could do to make her see that my relationship with her was, by then, as perfect as I thought it to be. Her mind was made up. The fact that there was ever something I did not accept about her, even though momentarily, was NOT something she would accept.

I simply stepped out of her life, as she demanded. Meanwhile, that book was then left hanging from a lie, with me unwilling to tell the readers a truth that was too personal to admit.

After a few years more, I settled with rewriting and adding a fictional side story . . . one that represented the wreck my life was in at the time but that had a fictional woman who portrayed the woman I truly know is out there looking for me. Yes, I KNOW there is a woman who will love me—love me for being exactly who I am.

As for our failed marriage? I gritted my teeth and admitted the true issue that initially hung me up from that perfect relationship—something I was neglecting to mention in the book. A stupid, little, insignificant something that I delt with by accepting it as being part of who she was.

Like in my childhood, I ate the asparagus that always gave me the dry heaves. I ate it because I had to. As an adopted child in Bingham Canyon, Utah, that lesson was clear. I had to in order to have a place to live. Likewise, I put up with this about my second wife. Did I accept this as being part of her? No. While she couldn't see the love that drove it, still, that was a lie.

So, you see, the book is, in reality, a love story that has not yet been consummated. Now you know about the inside story. The real question? Is there a woman who will accept me without the need to change anything? My own lesson being, will I likewise accept her, unconditionally, as I once did my first wife?

My second wife? Yes, I came to accept her—I thought. But no, she was right. I was only lying to myself. It, the thing I originally didn't accept . . . I only divorced IT as not being who she was. I could live with IT. But like that asparagus that still gives me the dry heaves, I was making HER acceptable. IT never was.

That fictional side story is the part that begs the question: Do I have to die to discover that perfect soul mate? Indeed, it would seem so. But NO. *I am the creator of my life, and I deserve it all.*

Questions:
- Does it bother you that I didn't tell you what "IT" was?
- It isn't a secret. I do tell it all in the novel. If it bothers you, are you going to just be pissed off—or what?

Action:
- ➤ This lesson was absolutely AWESOME for me. Consider making it so for you, too.

Skin Deep?

Y'know, fellas, ya gotta watch out when you're dealing with a woman. They can be pretty devious. In fact, seems the prettier they are, the more devious they are. It's like they think they've gotta protect themselves—from YOU! Does that make them prettier? Or uglier than what that devious shit does?

Playing those games of control is not a pretty thing to do. She may want to play them. But no matter how pretty the woman, those games always turn ugly. Pass her by. Her beauty is likely only skin deep.

The inner beauty of a woman seldom survives such beauty on the outside. The paint of society's façade isn't always pink. If that mascara-deep beauty is your requirement, you are only fucking yourself.

As for your own façade, once a woman sees your dishonesty, it won't matter if she's pretty or not on the inside or the outside. She won't be fucking you.

All this from the FACT that our society has taught us all—AND demanded—that we wear that façade, that lie. The truth of who you are may not be pretty to everyone, but it will be to some—the ones who can, and will, love you. Unless you show up as who you are, you will never know who those people are.

Questions:
- Does it make it hard for you, knowing that so few even want to know the truth of you, given your lie is showing them who they want you to be?
- Do you prefer honest acceptance to pretense?
- Do you long to meet someone who actually knows the difference?

Action:
➤ Choose.

PART SIX
Sexuality

If you want a loving relationship there can be NO fear. The two energies do NOT coincide. With love, or without it, sex is something we do because we enjoy it.

<u>**NOTE:**</u>

This next section may get some judgmental asses in an uproar. Keep in mind that it is outside the monogamous box most religions have taught you to stay in. Out beyond that, there is another box ruled by your fears. Do you remember how there is no right or wrong? There is loving and not loving. Loving does NOT require monogamy. Sex is NOT love, but whatever part it plays in your life, your life itself needs always be done in the energy of love—together or separately—with your partner.

Sex

Sex may—or may NOT—be done in the space of love. This is the law. But what does it mean?

When done in love, sex is one of the highest expressions of OUR love for one another. Outside of the higher unconscious energies of our soul, we only know, and physically feel, our own love.

Sex for your partner may be expressed in love or fear. Until you get to know them intimately, you DON'T know that. And some significant others will never let you in there that close.

I loved my wives—both of them. In that, my love was pure. But there was occasionally fear with my first wife. About once a month, she'd demand a divorce. Then it became about my fear of losing her.

For me now, I have to question just how much of that fear bled over into the rest of our life together. Love is an either/or thing, y'know. The energy of love and the energy of fear never coexist.

Now I question if my fear affected her love for me. And how much did it affect my ability to let her into that space of intimacy? Yes, her love was about security. I was her security in life. And that is fear. Was there ever a time when her love, too, was pure? It's really fucked up, but I'll never know.

Questions:
- Is it becoming clear to you just how complicated we humans make of the energy of our love and the energy of our fear?
- Do you see how seriously fucked up that can be?

Action:
- ➢ Always choose love. It is its own reward.

>>><<<

Love or Fear

Most people have this fear that their partner might "cheat"—have sex with someone else. That is about our OWN fear. That fear in us then makes it impossible to have love in our own life.

But consider this: There are some folks who deliberately have sex with other people out of pure love for one another.

- ❖ It may be that the guy has a small penis and he wants her to experience enjoying a BIG dick.
- ❖ Possibly, both want to see and experience watching one another getting some "strange."
- ❖ Or maybe they are into a polymorphic relationship with several partners at the same time.
- ❖ Could be that one is impotent but loves the other and wants them to get this need met.
- ❖ Hell, it could be they both just love having sex and don't give a fuck who they are having it with.
- ❖ And kink—sometimes one has a sexual kink the other doesn't have.
- ❖ Is that kink maybe that you just enjoy watching the other fuck? Do any of the above have to be a bad thing, an unloving thing?

Questions:
- • Did you find that something in this discussion was uncomfortable for you to think about?
- • You DO realize how that is about your fear, don't cha?
- • Does your fear keep you from discussing your needs with your partner?
- • How about intimacy? Does your fear prevent you from being intimate with them?

- How about acceptance? If you don't accept one another unconditionally, can there even BE love?
- Are you getting an understanding that love is an all-or-nothing thing?
- Which element of this discussion do you need to share intimately with your significant other?
- And now the BIG question: Do any of these issues stop you from loving them?
- How about them loving you?

Actions:

➤ Remember, right and wrong exist ONLY between someone's ears who has a judgmental mind. It does NOT exist out here in the real world.

➤ Have the courage to get honest with your significant other. Maybe they'll get honest with you, too.

➤ Tell them about all your sexual fantasies. You might both enjoy a vacation on Fantasy Island, whether you actually go there or not.

➤ Monogamy is generally a religious demand. But take away fear, and the alternate sexual possibilities are endless.

>>><<<

Sexual Energy

Spiritual Law #3—*Thoughts are energy.*

In being our own Creator, we choose, in every second of life, the energy with which we are creating. It can only be one of two energies—the energy of all that is love, or the energy of all that is not love (fear).

Both are contagious, and both infect those close by. One acts as a disease, the other, the cure. When it comes to the energy, there are many diseases. There is only the one cure.

Sex, too, is a thing of ecstasy when performed by two people in the energy of love. When performed in the energy of that which
is NOT love (fear), it comes in many forms—rape, abuse, cheating, degradation, molestation, pornography, masochism, and jealous payback. You get the picture. Not much of that would be termed as positive.

Questions:
- Has sex always been an act of love in your life?
- If that answer was "yes," don't cha think it's time to quit bullshitting yourself?
- Can you agree that sex is probably the most abused subject in the history of mankind—womankind, too?
- Even so, can you see sex as being in the space of love when it is done simply for mutual gratification?
- Why not? Is religion stinking up your judgment?

Actions:
- ➢ Stay in the space of love, personally, no matter what sex is to you as a single person or a couple.
- ➢ Remember, there is no right or wrong. There is only the energy of love and of everything that is not love. As a couple, no matter how you go about your sexuality, do it in the energy of love.
- ➢ You have heard this energy thing about love and fear multiple times. Has attaching it to sex given rise to seeing sex differently? Write about it.

Kinky

Everything about sex has been taught and rated as to what is acceptable by society and what is not—the good, the bad, and the ugly. Did you catch the earlier section about "good and bad?" How it doesn't exist outside of someone's judgmental mind? Yours maybe?

Kinky is just one of those things that society would put in the bad or ugly categories. It's about the stick that your individual society has stuck up its ass to hold its nose up into the air.

Where sex is concerned, I think it wise to change the rating to what uplifts one's spirit and what tears it down—what's loving or not. Or maybe, what is physically damaging and what is not, as in a matter of survival.

Funny thing is, what's loving usually depends on YOUR energy, and NOT what the sexual activity actually is. It could even be different for each, depending if the energy of the couple is different. Or, more to the point, depending on their individual judgments of right and wrong.

Kinky is generally the action that revolves around something one finds irresistible, at least in one's mind—fantasies and fetishes.

- ❖ The flavor of a woman's taco.
- ❖ The smell of someone's hair.
- ❖ Or if that hair has, or has not, been removed from a woman's holiest of holy hole.
- ❖ Having sex wearing comic animal costumes.
- ❖ Pegging—using a strap-on up the guy's ass. Usually, it's for the guy's pleasure, but some women like switching from the fuckee to being the fucker. Payback, maybe, or fun. You decide.

❖ Toys—much more fun when you have someone to operate the toy for you.

And then there's the heavy-duty weird shit.

❖ The taste of one's partner's toe juice.
❖ The smell and taste when running one's tongue around or in the other's anus.
❖ Scatt.
❖ Masochism—tying up, whips, and chains. Domination.
❖ Cock cages—denying him while she has her fun, usually with someone else.

Everything in this last section is either unhealthy or degrading.

❖ Watersports? Not so much. Unless there is an infection, urine has pretty much been sterilized naturally by the body. Of course, on the outside, it will mess with the sweet scent of a woman. Inside, it'll give a pussy some really bad breath.

I've barely scratched the itch on this nut sack. It appears there is no end to sexuality and our species' ability to come up with weird shit.

For me? I really enjoy a good taco. And toys? They can prolong sex for any woman well past the time any man's meat can remain useful.

Questions:
• What about you? List any kink you might have that I've not mentioned.
• Can yours be classed as healthy or unhealthy?
• How about love or fear—for you, of course?
• How about for them?

Actions:
- ➢ Tell your partner about your kinkiest fantasy. It might blow your relationship out of the water. Or it could open up sensuous realms and experiences well beyond anything you would likely ever experience together otherwise.
- ➢ Fantasies have a habit of becoming dishonest realities. Most people cheat when they don't believe they'll be acceptable at their kinkiest.
- ➢ Give yours the benefit of honesty.
- ➢ What I'm saying here is, get vulnerable. A lie is still a lie when it is one of omission. You are who you are. They aren't worthy of being in your life if they won't accept the "real" you—and that wind blows both ways.

The Tale of the Stick

As I get older, one thing I've come to realize is that most women my age have the idea ingrained in them that all a man wants is to get his willy wet by her. I suppose it doesn't help when I talk and joke openly about sex.

But hey, I'm not into changing anyone's mind to suit me. Nor will I change from being open and honest about myself just to suit them.

If I did—if I wore that façade expected of me—don't they see that who I am would be a lie? And when the truth dawns on them, as it will eventually, it'll hurt. But then, that is just the way society has taught us all to be—dishonest.

Do I then want to believe or trust that she is being honest with me? Can I possibly believe she doesn't wear a façade of her own? Not when all I see in her is a woman who pulled the stick out of her ass just long enough to beat me with it.

I suppose the only way I can know for sure is if a woman comes along who doesn't pull out her stick and try to hit me with the shitty end just for being me. I'm still waiting for that woman.

Questions:
- Do you see the whole fake thing about façades that society demands of everyone? Not many folks do, y'know.
- Do you feel I've explained it well enough?
- Or do people just refuse to see it? Yeah, that would require them to change their minds.
- And yeah again. Their whole fucking life would then change. Fear of change is a coward's reason for not looking.

Action:
- ➤ If this strikes home for you, I'm asking that you do your own FUCKING thinking.

>>><<<

Female ED—Loss of Libido

I may have lost my ability physically in the dick department, but I have not lost it in the mental—the gray matter—department. I would still want to satisfy my woman sexually, regardless.

Despite sex, relationships are about the meeting of needs. To truly love someone, one must meet those needs simply on the strength of one's love. So, what's my need? Right now, it's to be a man in the sexuality department.

So, the question is: Does my woman want the love I offer, taking sexual satisfaction with what a male lesbian can offer, and stay together? Or does she want to get her sex handled separately—to love me in her heart while she fucks someone else? In a relationship, solutions are a two-party thing, something that we can't control alone.

Remember, needs will trump all in a relationship. Some women need sexual satisfaction delivered with man meat alone, no matter how fleetingly it is given. Others just need to be loved and would welcome a man to join her in her toy department.

Pain is the guaranteed human condition whenever life isn't the way we want it. Yeah, I've known such pain and don't want to pass it on.

I have shared all this from a man's—my own—point of view. I'm not capable of sharing it from a woman's. If you have it in you to do, or not do, sex in the space of love, I can make a few suggestions from a man's perspective.

If you are a woman with female ED, there are men who prefer oral to vaginal intercourse. Some even prefer anal as well. There is also fantasizing—verbally sharing all your kinky thoughts and/or experiences of having sex with someone else.

Just being in a relationship does NOT mean you own one another. When we come into this world, all we have is life and a little time to live it. Respect one another's autonomy to live their life as they see fit without your interference. Deciding to be a couple does not give you the right of ownership.

If owning your partner is where your joy is, get a dog. They may not be as much fun sexually—and then they may—but they are always good companions.

If, as a couple, your minds are truly liberated . . . out beyond all rules of society or religion, there is freedom. Many of society's rules result in petty jealousies. Most do not deal kindly with ED.

Like some men, a woman's lack of libido may be connected to a lack of excitement—no risk of getting caught satisfying one's nasty, little fantasies. Some couples are into sharing. Just the fact that what you are doing is socially unacceptable can help drive some folks' sexuality. If it does no physical harm, why not.

There is the concept of cuckoldry—one person getting off on watching the other having sex with someone outside the relationship. Sex alone is not love. Some find great satisfaction in being a part of experiencing the other's adventures, or misadventures.

Then there is polyamory—more than two people making up the relationship.

Doing these kinds of things sexually *requires* trust and acceptance and, most of all, honesty. Much more so than most folks are willing to do. Of course, society and religion call it wrong, but is it? Again, right and wrong exist only in the shit between your ears. It does NOT exist in reality.

Sex is a need. It can be a part of, but alone, it is not love. Sex is an intimate act, a personal thing. You do it for your own gratification. When doing it in a loving relationship, it then needs to be about the gratification of both.

If sex is not always done with honesty, it is as much your doing as it is theirs. If you don't have open honesty with one another, you don't have acceptance and trust. Without those two things, you are only lying to yourself about love.

Honesty takes courage. Sometimes who you are sexually is not acceptable by who they are. That does not mean you have to part. Where sex is concerned, you can go your separate ways and still be in a loving relationship, but that requires you to discuss it honestly with one another and find an acceptable solution.

Thing is, you don't know without honesty. This is where our society, with its lying façades, fucks you up. Our religions, with their stick-up-the-ass lies about what God wants, do the same. Those lies are why people are afraid to be honest and is the biggest reason for cheating.

As is the fear they may have of your judgmental mind. Everyone has a need to be respected, revered, cherished, and loved. That is all covered under accepted.

Questions:
- Have you ever been in a relationship where there was just one little thing you did not accept about them?
- I have. Read **Somewhere Out There** in Part Five. The full story is in Chapter Thirty-three of **The Soul of an Eagle**. Do you see how it fucked me in the ass on my way out of that marriage?

Actions:
- ➤ *There is LOVE and there is everything that is not love (FEAR).* Spiritual Law #3, again. The two energies do not coexist. If you are afraid of your mate's judgments of you, it is an all-the-time thing. As far as your relationship goes, your fear will fuck you in the ass—every time. **Write about that**.
- ➤ Then have the courage to be honest with your mate. You don't know how she, or he, will take it, but do you really want to keep on trucking down this road, hoping that when it ends, it will be in a less painful place? It won't.

>>><<<

PART SEVEN
Politics

So, okay. When it comes to the Liberal wokey-doke crowd, it's like trying to split pubic hairs. Splitting hairs is one thing, but kinky, curly pubic hairs are an exercise in futility. And yeah . . . I have huge difficulty in keeping my pubes from being in a major uproar—especially when my current love interest runs screaming into the night because I voted for Trump.

Clusterfuck

Is there anything more fucked over by the rules of society than *sexuality*? Yeah, that's no longer gospel. These days, "fucking over" is the new job of politics.

For a while, what with society's morality rules and religion's judgmental mind, it looked like we were being told not to procreate.

Then along came this current Covid 19 plandemic, coupled with all the money and power behind this vaccine—which doesn't work—that caused me to wonder about the reality of it all.

Fauci and Gates both have publicly come out in favor of reducing the world's population. And both have been in the thick of this situation with the Wuhan lab from which the virus "escaped." So, in the political arena of our society, it is now a fact—politics is running the show now, and they definitely do NOT want us to procreate.

But then, every wannabe, little, despotic politician with a smidgeon of power and a hard-on decided to make mandates into royal edicts. Yeah, they started forcing people to be vaxed.

But the vaccines didn't stop people from getting Covid, remember? Oh, shit! We need to mandate that those who had Covid, and survived, need to be vaccinated to protect those already vaxed with a vaccine that doesn't work.

Huh? B-b-but what about natural immunity? Yeah, you got it.

CLUSTERFUCK!

I warned you that this book would go redneck deep into all of it—spirituality and its laws, relationships, religion, sexuality, politics—all things considered socially untouchable.

Here it cums! The clusterfuck that is now . . . POLITICS.

Questions:
- What do YOU consider as things one should never talk about in public?
- Is that because you want to avoid the fervor some Liberal has about being "right"?
- Is your thinking any "righter?" Or is it just functional, being based on the truths of life—Spiritual Laws.

Actions:
- ➢ Before you offer them your opposing view, ask yourself, "Is it worth swimming upstream in their cesspool when you are just another stupid turd to them?"
- ➢ My God, where does one go for sanity when the whole world has gone insane? Locking yourself in your house almost seems to make sense.

Not a Pretty Sight

Do you remember me telling you about what taking offense is about? How it makes you a victim when it is only based on your feelings? And how NOT taking offense when it is based on something actually physically harmful to you ALSO makes you a victim? What this Biden Administration is doing to my country, THAT is actually harmful to my life—and it is ALSO about my feelings.

I am a vet. I took the oath to protect The Constitution from enemies foreign AND domestic. Every move this administration has made has been to the detriment to our country. That can't be an accident. So yes, it is definitely about my feelings, and about my honor, that I take offense. And yes, I have very little love to offer. What to do?

I'm going to get real honest—naked even—shave my pubes, and just let my feelings hang out. This section is NOT a pretty sight.

The dishonesty and brutality of this plandemic is a *given* ... the actions that our own and other governments have levied upon the people worldwide is a *given* . . . the millions of people who have needlessly died when there were cures readily available is a *given*. Lastly, it is also a *given* that I would be extremely dishonest not to say the truth about it—brutal or not. I know this won't come across as loving. It is just reeee-ul difficult to love someone who is tearing down your country. *Forgive me of my humanity.*

Questions:
- How do YOU feel about it all?
- Are you doing anything to fight?

Actions:
- ➢ What are you doing? Tell it to yourself.
- ➢ Me? Why do you think I wrote this fucking book—and why it has so many F-bombs? Throw a few yourself.

Loving Myself

It's true. I've not had much to say that is loving about the Democratic Socialist Party of America—The Fourth Reich. Am I breaking Spiritual Law #3? I don't believe so.

Thoughts are energy.

In being our own Creator, we choose, in every second of life, the energy with which we are creating. It can only be *one* of *two* energies: the energy of *all that is love* or the energy of *all that is not love* (fear).

Both are contagious, and both infect those close by. One acts as a disease, the other, the cure. When it comes to the energy, there are many diseases. There is only the one cure.

Telling the truth IS loving. Telling lies—and believing them—is NOT. The Liberals of the Fourth Reich tell a shitload of lies. And fear energy? They've managed to make a clean break from anything loving. The energy of fear spews out of the left side of government like explosive diarrhea. Yes, we are a divided country, now more so than ever.

It was bad enough when the divide was between the North and South. There were loving people on both sides of that conflict. But the left and right sides now?

I am hard-pressed to see ANYBODY who is loving, and on the left—certainly not on the far-left end. Seems those in the middle have left the party.

So, love? Where is, or was, there love in my life?

There was my first wife. I loved her dearly. Yet all I could see in her was that I was simply her security in life and not much else. That was about her fear—not love. Still, maybe she did love me, but differently from the way I loved her. All I could see in her was her need to control. Control is the game we are all taught by most aspects of our society, and many see it as being their love.

But games cannot be played unless there are at least two parties playing. Like with war, it kinda demands two armies. And yes, I was playing her game. When I quit playing my part, there was nothing left that worked in our relationship, so we parted.

I recently entered into a relationship. We had so much fun doing life together. I thought it didn't matter that she was a Liberal. It was okay with me that we thought differently where politics was concerned. I just wanted us to love one another. And for my part, I did.

Her? I thought she did, too—until she found out I voted for Trump. The very thought of that sent her shittin' and gittin' into the night, all the while spewing political diarrhea back at me.

Yeah, if you want a loving relationship, you need to find someone who is loving. Is there anyone on the left who is? I dunno.

Me? That question goes to my own responsibility.

Questions:
- Am I someone who is loving?
- Or am I just blind to my fear?
- Is this loneliness I now feel about my fear?
- Or is it merely about being alone—and loving myself enough to be okay alone?

Action:
- ➤ I am going to enjoy this time being alone.

Your Wokey-Doke Kingdom

Your world consists of how you see everything, your perception. No one's world is the same, *ever*—guaranteed. If you are one of those folks in the wokey-doke crowd who insists that other people are responsible for how you choose to feel, then maybe it is time to realize that your perception of it is based on a lie—one that is fucking up your life royally.

I say "royally" to point out that you do not sit on a monarch's throne in anyone's life but your own. No one is your subject. No one lives their own life just to suit yours. *And no one is responsible for your choice of feelings, except you.*

Being a wokey-doke king in someone else's world is the lie that society has taught you. It does not serve you. Are you wondering why? Are you pissed off and taking offense that I would attack your world by saying such blasphemy to your royal highness?

Is it my job in my world to point out to you why your world isn't working for you? No, except maybe in that our own personal worlds don't need to collide. And what makes them do so are the lies we each insist on believing.

That is the crux of what personal growth is all about— searching out the lies that fuck up our lives. That is why I am able to help out simply by pointing you toward the truth, which begs the question: What makes my truth a royal decree in your kingdom?

Do you believe in the law of gravity? It's a physical law that will definitely fuck up your physical person if you disobey it, no matter which world you live in.

Is it conceivable that life itself might have its own rules—laws just as nonvolatile that govern? When we break those laws, our personal worlds do collide in uncomfortable ways. Why else would there be such violence between so many people's worlds?

If you have this wokey-doke thing going, you are breaking one of the greatest of all rules that govern life. It is the number one law that all of the others are taken from.

I am the Creator.

Only I can create my own life—you can't. Life is sovereign to each person. I have no right, or ability, to create how you perceive anything in your life. Perception, remember, is how every person creates their individual world. And perception is the choices you make about the beliefs in your mind—*your* choices, not mine.

This does not mean we can't communicate. I can tell you what works for me. After all, we are social creatures. But in the end, we all decide what works for ourselves. It is from the lie of wokeness that wars begin.

Questions:
- Why would your royal wokeness ever believe that you can break life's rules and not be dysfunctional? Wars do have a way of escalating. They always do when we have to be "right."
- What if there was no "right" or "wrong"?
- What if there were only what works and what does not?
- What if me telling you about these rules of life was not an assault on your world, but rather, a gift offered?
- Would you accept it?

Actions:
- ➤ Think about it. Yeah, do your own FUCKING thinking.
- ➤ Then take off that wokey-doke joker's cloak and throw it away. It doesn't suit you—or serve you.

Sniffing Stains or Ripping Scabs

Do you get the feeling that I am down on this whole "woke culture"? Or is it that "woke" is just the latest word defining what I am not? Could it be exactly so?

Again, the simple thing is, this world is one of duality—the *from* and *to* thing. This duality we are talking about here is the *from* and *to* of New Thought to Woke. They are at opposite ends of the spectrum of our thought systems. New Thought is about taking full responsibility in life. Woke is about taking none.

Responsibility—the ability to respond, and consequently, to be the absolute Creator of your life.

Woke is about abdicating that responsibility. It is about being a victim in life, unable to respond to anything. Does looking at me and all this "silly shit" I'm telling you really chap your ass?

Believe me, tasting the nectar of the peach is so much more satisfying than just licking the fuzz off the outside. Is that what I am like to you? Someone licking at the fuzz encasing your life? Is that fuzz the lies you would hide behind?

Or am I like the skid stains in someone's shorts? Or the ones I get on my ass whenever I fall off my motorcycle? I'm really not interested in exploring your shorts for stains any more than you are with picking the scabs off my ass.

But wait! Maybe factoring in that wokeness does feel like being violated to you. I gotta admit, the normal response I get from those in the WOKE is like me having the scabs ripped off my ass.

What if we were to slice it to the heart and let what's inside of you rub up against what's inside of me? Seems to me, that is what we both would enjoy doing a lot more.

Questions:
- Sniffing stains or ripping scabs . . . is that what we are doing?
- Wouldn't open honesty with what's inside be better?
- You rubbing what the truth is inside of you up against a like truth in me—wouldn't that be the most nurturing aspect possible in both our lives?

Action:
> We're not talking sex here, y'know. But hell, that might work, too. Does this smile make my face look fat? You don't have to answer that.

>>><<<

Politically Evil

Yes, while you possibly weren't looking, I've introduced you to several laws that may be dramatically opposed to your current beliefs, as well as others not so dramatic. For now, let's look at the evil at hand. But to do that, I need to bring up another Spiritual Law.

Law #50—What is of true evil in this life is created in your mind through the process of determining "what is good and what is bad"—and especially, in "what is right and wrong."

That's right. Evil is created by our own judgmental thoughts. Evil is just a tag, a sign we post concerning something we don't like that is usually harmful in the extreme. Often, the true source of that harm lies in ourself judging something that does no actual harm. So yes, I'll own the judgments I have personally about one particular evil . . . one I believe will do unimaginable harm to us all.

The current vaccines that we will soon be legally required—DEMANDED—to take.

They alter our DNA, the one thing that makes us everything we are. I'd say DNA is a thing bestowed by our Higher Power. *And it is being FUCKED OVER and CHANGED by these vaccines.* And even more so, our body's natural defenses to all manner of diseases are also being fucked with. This vaccine has already killed thousands of people—undeniably. From what some of those doctors who have cojones (look up "Front

Line Doctors") are saying, it will kill *everyone* who has taken "the jab" within a few short years.

Oh hey, I don't expect you to take my word for this, but you might invest the time to look at who is tied up with creating these vaccines. Then ask yourself how many are tied to funding the Chinese labs from which the Covid virus "escaped." You might also throw into consideration who is touting it, making money on it, AND, has publicly announced being in favor of *reducing the population of the world*. To slap you upside your face, here's the final question: There are a lot of stupid sheeple in this world. Are you one of them?

Does my sign say "THE WORLD IS COMING TO AN END"? Seems so. Will there be any survivors?

Well, sure. There are a lot of super-rich people who suddenly are buying their own private islands. And there are underground shelters for all the government psychopaths. And then there are all those radicals in places like Afghanistan. When the chaos reigns, they will likely kill one another off, but some will survive to become the new peasants existing in the new sixth century AD. It will make no difference to those rich overseers living in the new twenty-first or twenty-second centuries.

No, I don't expect ANYONE will believe this flight of fancy. It's really "out there." But then, it seems this whole world is hanging over the abyss. I expect a few who've taken the jab may believe it just enough to pose the question, "OMG! I've taken the damned vaccine. Isn't there *anything* I can do? What if all this proves true?"

Yeah, there is something you can do—PRAY. Which brings me to another Spiritual Law—*Law #35: We have absolute abundance, limited only by our belief in ourselves—in who we are—as an actual part of God.*

Despite being hijacked by multiple religions, *there is still that Higher Power* with an unlimited ability to create and fix anything. And prayer is mankind's way of seeking out that power. Meditation is another. Religions will tell you to first admit your "sin." I don't agree with the sin part—*that's just the judgmental shit from between the ears of organized religion.* But I do believe you have to get the lesson. You fucked up by believing in an administration that you *knew* was corrupt. You allowed them to "stick you," and you didn't even have to drop your shorts and bend over. They said they only wanted to stick you in the arm. *They lied.*

As for that Higher Power? Why would God expect you not to make mistakes? Although we do have a higher purpose, we are all—every one of us—here to learn the lessons of our souls. Those lessons are often sparked off by fuck ups, in part. Sin aside, on the simply spiritual soul side, it "just is." Working with that part of yourself—yeah, that part that is so much greater than you are consciously—*does* require honesty. You can't fix or change *anything* if you don't see and acknowledge the truth of it.

I currently have 3,108 friends on Facebook. It will be interesting to see how many of them will now take flight outta Kabul town here. When you are dealing with a reality like Kabul, taking a flight of fancy is usually not recommended—unless that reality

SUCKS just as bad. These vaccine jabs do, every bit as bad as this administration's handling of Kabul.

So, okay. I've been talking about those Spiritual Laws. If you've been listening, I expect you're getting a clue about what they are all about.

As I've said, they're the simple truths of life. Yet in a world filled with lies—lies designed for one person to control others—those lies form the perception with which most in this world perceive life. They are the light by which life is generally showcased. And still, they are lies, the dysfunctions by which most are crippled in life.

The Spiritual Laws, the simple truths, illuminate life differently—functionally—but very few ever grow spiritually enough to see by their light. For those who do, life is then something the others will never experience but all unknowingly want. Living life by the lies of others will always make one a victim.

So why discount the truth in favor of those lies? The truth has always been out there in everyone's face. Our soul inherently knows the truth. It spends your whole lifetime offering it up as lessons. The only benefit we get for *not* accepting those lessons is in abdicating our responsibilities. We get to blame, but we never get to be in control of our own lives.

How's that working for you?

And speaking of working for you, I need to know if this book series is working for anyone. If you are following . . . if these posts are adding anything to your life . . . I need to know that I am not just pissing into the wind. This isn't Facebook, but you can still throw a "like" to this by telling your friends. They might like it, too. Or better yet, write a review on Barnes and Noble online or on Amazon. It is usually fun to run in the rain—provided it IS rain. But hey, you can stop reading if you think it's not.

If you are like most people, you don't appreciate someone telling YOU how THEY see life differently. No problem. I am looking to connect with those who know something of the Spiritual Laws—or want to know.

Questions:
- What do you think?

- Is it, "Vax on, Daniel Son"?
- Or "Vax off"?

Actions:
> Write about what you consider is the most important aspect of this post.
> And of this book so far.

>>><<<

The Wokey-Doke of Critiques

Wow! This whole wokey-doke group in Liberal America—the Democratic ass-crack in government that has been shitting on the rest of us—have been taking their steroids. Seems it only takes one in any group to bitch and moan loud enough to shut out anyone with whom they disagree.

I dunno what it will take before the rest of us stop taking their shit and allowing ourselves to be held ransom to their itty-bitty fweelings. Personally, I think it is about time the rest of us grew a set. Whaddaya think?

YEAH, this time, it's got my redneck up. I am taking *huge* offense. This time, it IS affecting my quality of life physically.

I just received an email from one of the two critique groups I still belong to. I've gone through every major writers' critique group in town. I'm on the last one now. The reason is always the same: The woke culture always finds a way of silencing anyone who disagrees with them.

Those of us who are New Thought, and especially those on the Right, simply don't feel the need to try to change their minds to agree with ours. Hell, it's not even about agreeing, rather, about accepting and being accepted. It's not functional to try and change others, nor is it our right. As for me, I can accept them—that does not mean I want to be around them.

Right now, this is the only book I'm writing, and I won't be censured. Will anyone in the woke ever see the truth and wake up? Funny how so many on the left are so fearfully fixated on being *right*? For me, the game of control is one I don't play.

What follows is my resignation from the group. I just now emailed it to them, and here it is, almost verbatim.

Folks,

Every critique group I've been in has maintained they are about critiquing the writing and not the content. Then, all but the last one turned around and let their one or two wokey-doke members bully them.

Your affiliate, the HWG, is the only one that hasn't— YET. And maybe they will. Tomorrow's reading is a continuation of this last one, the one you are censuring.

I'm not sure if it was them or you who recently had a reader who went to extremes with bashing on the Trump crowd. And hey, I voted for Trump, but I said nothing. I recognized that person had a right to think however he wants and to write whatever he chooses. However, I am curious. Did anyone break a woke on him? Or send a letter suggesting he shut-the-fuck-up?

No matter. Like with those other critique groups, I didn't take offense—and don't now—or demand others live their lives or think any differently than they do, just to suit me. That would be against the Spiritual Laws, not to mention everything I stand for as a veteran.

The woke culture ALWAYS prefers to take offense, then blames others for a choice they, themselves, made in their fweelings. Bottom line: Their dysfunction didn't work with mine. Like your other conservative members, I choose not to be the butt of your wokey-doke discord. And I have the cojones to tell you clearly.

With the other groups, I simply recognized that I didn't fit in and left—just as I do now with you. Like you, they were trying to censure my material. Only one group actually kicked me out.

But to be censured? Why would I allow some snowflake wanna-be dictator tell me what to do in creating my life? Like every red-blooded American, *I am its creator*. So long as I pose no harm to others, I won't capitulate. I won't give others the power to run my life. This is what living that first Spiritual Law means.

Even so, I have always felt that my association with those other critique groups, and yours, has enriched me as a writer. While their critiques were often more like attacks, I learned a lot about myself as a writer.

I sincerely wish you all the best.

Egorhh

Questions:
- Do you just see me as a victim, bitching and moaning?
- Or maybe a veteran honoring his oath to the Constitution?
- How about someone standing up for his rights without committing violence as the Liberals so often do?

Actions:
- You gotta know that the choice is coming to your own life.
- When it does, don't you wonder if violence might then be the only choice you can have and still call yourself a man?

All Lives Matter

"Black Lives Matter." Is it the battle cry of racial equality or the whimper of someone demanding the rights to their victimhood? Is it saying a black life is every bit as important as yours—no matter what color yours is?

Isn't that the same thing as, "Please recognize me as a member of your species because how you see me is *much* more important to me than how I see me. For black people, doesn't this whole movement stink of a clusterfuck of insecure people who see themselves as victims?

And then there are a lot of whites and all the other minorities in the BLM marches/riots. All it says to me is that they buy into the drama. BLM has succeeded in guilt-tripping them. They, too, accept that they have victimized you, whereas in truth, we only victimize ourselves.

But then, doesn't saying "Black Lives Matter" actually imply that black is the only color of life that matters? Gotta wonder about that one when experiencing the angst reflected whenever someone states what is taken as a conflicting opinion that *"all lives matter."* That statement could get you killed if uttered at a BLM rally.

What is the truth of it, if not a statement of victimhood? "You have made me a victim, and now you're gonna pay." Are you not calling me a racist while ignoring the bottom-line truth of your own racism? WHY? C'mon, what purpose does it serve if not to demand victimhood due to being black, no matter what your own color?

When will we evolve far enough to see that life is a function of intelligence, of consciousness, bottom line of sentience? It only concerns what a person creates in his or her own life. Nothing else means shit.

I've heard it said that dolphins are every bit as intelligent as humans, just in a different way. Could that be true? But wait! Don't human fishermen kill thousands of them every year when caught up in their fishing nets? Would that give dolphins the right to march in, say, "Dolphin Lives Matter" parades?

No, wait . . . shit, I forgot! They can't march, can they? And dolphins rioting? They probably wouldn't know about starting fires any better than an octopus can write love letters with the ink from its asshole.

I suppose we'll just have to wait until some alien species comes along. Sure . . . then you'll have to let go of that silly battle cry—Black Lives Matter—and join together as human beings fighting against alien enslavement.

I guess the real question is: Why do we humans always see ourselves as "less than" so that we need to fight amongst ourselves? And the aliens? It's a good bet they will originally come in peace, and we humans just didn't think that *they* thought *we* were good enough to be their friends. We'd rather see ourselves as being their victims. Isn't "less than" just another way of saying "victim"?

C'mon, folks! This whole stupid, fucking drama is based on how *we* think *others* perceive us. As for the truth? *"Thoughts create."* That is the law applied here. We are who we think we are. Most of us want to be victims in life just to relieve ourselves of the responsibility of that one big kahuna of a Spiritual Law that says, *"I am the Creator."* (I am the responsible party in my life.)

Spiritual Laws are only the simple truths of life, remember? And yes, I am aware that disagreeing with the BLM wokey-doke crowd might just rile a few of them up—make them want to beat me up, bend me over, and wokey-pokey me. But you gotta know that doing that to anyone who disagrees with you would just be a really shitty thing to do. Accepting that others have the right to disagree is not only the American way, it's also a good way to keep the shit off your wokey-pokey stick.

Questions:
- Do you buy into the whole guilt trip called Black Lives Matter?
- Do you feel ashamed of being a different color and join in the riots?
- If so, do you consider yourself as human?
- Or does what some dimwit of an ancestor did mean more to you than what you are doing?
- Because if you are rioting in the name of Black Lives Matter, hurting other people, how can you consider yourself human?

Action:
- ➤ Get a fucking grip on yourself. Have some fucking respect for others—no matter what their fucking color. (Is that emphasized enough in redneck speak?)

Children's No Fossil Fuel Proliferation Pact?

I just received a notice on Facebook from *Sierra* magazine. Dunno what you think about it, but I'm calling it bullshit. The fact that they put it in terms of our "children's" No Fossil Fuel Proliferation Pact makes it even worse. It's as disgusting as bullshit gets.

It seems that is what Liberal Americans like to do—drag their own stool out of the toilet of their mind and present that shit as coming from our sweet, innocent children.

Speaking of facts, here is one I once heard expressed by a scientist, one who, I expect, would know.

FACT:
There are more greenhouse gas emissions blown into the atmosphere by just one volcano than have ever been put there by man in the entire time he's been on this planet.

NOW:
Take that thought and count up the number of active, spewing volcanoes there were just in this last year. I think man's allotment for the rest of eternity has been filled, even given the unlikely circumstance that mankind may live as long as Earth has left in the duality—its *from* and *to* on this plane of existence. Such is not even the smallest of farts stinking up the infinite essence of eternity.

JUST TO COMPARE:
The total lifetime of mankind to this present moment would compare to the time the first dinosaur spent before hatching out of its shell. It is said that the span of the dinosaurs went from January 1st through the third week in September. Mankind's started on December 31st.

NOW:
Your "Green New Deal" is NOTHING to this earth's existence. To mankind, it's an embarrassing travesty, not to be confused with a fart, but rather as explosive diarrhea where your very guts spew out. Give this one to those fake, fucking fact-checkers at Liberal Facebook!

Questions:
- Do you believe the Green New Deal bullshit?

- Do you see how this whole Covid thing has been planned just to get us used to giving up our freedoms?
- If that is part of the plan, what part do you suspect this god-awful, expensive Green New Deal is tailored to do?
- Break America financially? Maybe?
- Talk about the deep state elites. What will it take to resist them—or stop them? They're running a scam called the "One World Government."

Action:
- ➢ Be ready to pay the price. I suspect that for most of us, the price will be our lives.

Blind, Fake, or Stupid

This *Redneck Spirituality* series of books is based on truth—the Spiritual Laws are the simple truths of life. And the truth about life is that it is *only* the lies that make it dysfunctional. Speaking of dysfunctional, *blame* is always a lie.

As for thought systems, there are those who take full responsibility in their lives, and there are those who blame. This has no political lines. There are both types of people in both parties. So how does politics play ANY part in it?

Here is another thought: Maybe thought systems and belief systems are not the same thing. There are only two belief systems—those who believe what those in authority say and those who think for themselves and form their own beliefs. This does *not* cut across both political parties. Where the Liberal Democrats are concerned, what the authority, the party, says is gilded in gold. It is not to be questioned. No one has the right to think for themselves.

And no one in the Democratic Party is *not* a Liberal. It is pretty hard to think for one's self and not see the truth. Those in authority—whether knowingly or unknowingly—blame the other party for every underhanded thing they, themselves, are about. *That is play number one in the Liberal playbook.*

Those outside of the leadership have only three choices to pick from in calling themselves a Democrat: BLIND, FAKE, or STUPID.

This explains why they aren't allowed to think for themselves. They'd have to be blind not to see the lie in blame or fake not to care. Or simply stupid not to understand that they, themselves—the party's base—could make their whole party functional.

Questions:
- Are you a Liberal Democrat?
- If you are *still* reading this now, you may think of yourself as a Democrat—but a Liberal? No fucking way.
- Are you Blind? Fake? Or stupid? No, you'd have to be a brain-dead Democrat to get this far in this book.

Action:
➢ Vote Republican. You can do that as an Independent.

The Woking Dead

Woke culture is bent on taking their victim dramas to the extremes. They try to paint everything and everyone with the color of negativity, all in the name of racism. Give me a fucking break! Did these people all get lobotomies?

Who is it that is forcing such negativity to spew out of them with every breath? Which end are they talking out of anyway? How do so many people turn into such whining, crybaby victims to everything in this world?

Surely, this is the result of some viral plague, unbeknownst to those who are sickened with it. It simply cannot be coming from an act of willful misery on their own part. Ah, such drama!

But wait. Drama is always about control. The need to conform everybody and everything within one's personal existence, to bend them to one's own superior will, to force those others to live only to suit your own royal wokeness is nothing short of blindly abusing one's royal edicts. A fellow by the name of Bill Whittle recently summed them up under the term "The Woking Dead."

I don't know who coined the term, but I would add "... dead in the head." That is, dead to the thought of creating their own life as they would want it to be. Y'gotta know, controlling others has never been a functional way to create your own life, whereas controlling one's own self is.

For me, being a vet, "the head" is actually a military term describing the outhouse—like the one at Rumi's Field. And the shit coming from between one's ears is as diarrhea spewing out of one's mouth.

Question:
- My only hope is that your head isn't too big. Does it fit into that wooden hole?

Action:
➤ Don't miss.

Just Shining a Light Up Your Ass

Gotta say that this whole "WOKE" thing is about the simple-minded. It's merely a word used to describe someone who likes to take offense.

What makes it simple-minded? Offense is something that must be TAKEN. It is not something GIVEN, no matter what YOU say or do. Simple, wouldn't you say?

As for you? Taking offense is just one of those things you do toward other people akin to dropping your pants, bending over, and spreading your cheeks. It is just YOU literally showing the whole world a genuine ASSHOLE.

Who else besides the Woking Deadheads would make themselves a victim by taking offense with you, then blame you for their own lack of honesty by not taking responsibility for their own choice of feelings?

Questions:
- So many folks get reeee-ul hung up on blaming others for their feelings. Are you one of them?
- No? Okay, then. WERE you one of them?

Action:
> DON'T EVER DO THAT AGAIN!

>>><<<

Duality

Oh, the duality of life . . . Truth is, one can never appreciate how wonderful life can be if they never experience how shitty it occasionally is.

To compare the true essence of the finest of life's great cuisine, it must be matched against the reality of one's own cooking and the diarrhea that may sometimes result.

Seems that in these last couple of years, all I could get my hand around was the shitty end of the Covid stick. But a fella's gotta wonder who was holding the other end of that stick—and whose shit is on it.

From the way my sphincter's been clutched up all this time, I expect it was mine. The deep state has been in charge of reaming the freedom out of us all.

No doubt that with the installation of Biden's Socialist Party, complete with all of its free perks and extravagant spending, one can only wonder about when the explosion begins in one's pants.

As for those pants? That kind of embarrassment has no match. It is the very pits where Patriotism is concerned when knowing one's country is run by . . . and running with . . . shit.

I know the shelves are emptied of TP, but not to worry. Biden's freshly printed currency will make excellent toilet paper.

Questions:
- Just so, will Biden's presidency mark the end of all the greatness of these United States?
- Will the rest of the world be required to hold its nose while trying not to laugh?

Action:
- ➤ The time will come. When it does—FIGHT FOR OUR FREEDOMS!

The Sign of the Devil?

I saw a picture of some sculpturer's rendition of the devil giving "the sign." It was alongside of a picture of Fauci giving the same sign.

Hmmm . . .

Sometimes ya just gotta reveal yourself. Is that what Fauci was doing? I've heard it said that the Higher Power has some kind of a rule that says people have to warn you about the truth of who they are, but they don't always do so out loud or in a way most folks will hear them and take it seriously. Personally, I think who a person is will always show, at some time, unconsciously in their actions.

Do you believe that, as the Bible states, God is omnipotent—everywhere, within everything? The simple truth about this earthly existence is that everything always exists as a duality. All the energy is of God—the good, loving energy as is the not-so-loving "evil" energy. God is everywhere within everything, the full scope of it all. The good, the bad, and the evil? Those are just our own judgments from within our own minds—not God's.

I also believe that God, like mankind, prefers the sweet to the sour, the love to the evil. And as I said, He requires *everyone* to tell others who they are. For the most part, when the loving, good folks tell you, you usually believe and sometimes are surprised when later you find they misled you. But somewhere along the line, I believe they DID, indeed, tell you the truth. You just didn't see or hear it.

Bottom line: That full gamut of the energy resides within us all. Who we are being, the energy in which we most generally choose to reside, is our choice.

Here we have Fauci, a very respectable figure in a position of extreme authority (supposedly good). In this picture, is he telling you the truth about who he is? That may well be so, but then, that is just my own personal beliefs, most of which are based on all his actions.

Are you FUCKING listening?

Now, do you think that ME, lobbing this F-bomb at YOU, makes ME evil? Truth is, "evil" is not found anywhere except in YOUR judgmental mind—and mine. Actions are just actions . . . sometimes loving, sometimes not.

"Fucking" is an action and a fact of life. In fact, there would not BE any life without it. But it IS something people often judge as somehow "evil." Therefore, it is a word they perk up and hear, which makes it a redneck's special "slap-you-upside-your-head" word.

It's the actions that are loving, and those that are not, to which one needs to pay attention. Is it that picture of him giving that sign, or the fact that he supplied the funds to the Wuhan lab where the Covid 19 virus strain was created? And then there is the fact that Fauci has made a shitload of money off this plandemic and gained immense power from it as well.

Which action speaks loudest to you? Whether you believe there is a law (about good and evil), or the reality of one's actions (about loving or not), Fauci is showing you who he is. Yes, he was a major actor in funding the Wuhan lab and in the vaccine that doesn't work. That says to me that a lot of people died due to Fauci and this plandemic. I'd say his actions say it all, don't cha think?

Questions:
- There have been many people who, down through history, have changed this world—some for the better, some for the worst. Which category would you say Fauci is in?

- Why?
- Do you think he deserves a commendation?
- Or do you think this world would be better were he never in it?

Action:

- ➤ Write down your thoughts on him and send them to your government leaders. Never mind the news services or social media. For the most part, they are no longer viable resources.

>>><<<

Jive Talkin'

You know, or perhaps you don't, we are all the same on that higher spiritual level. We all have a soul made of the same stuff—*God stuff*. I suppose that coming from a white, redneck culture, that knowledge sets me apart in a minority . . . a minority within a minority . . . one for which we are now expected to be ashamed.

Sad because that *God stuff* is the bottom line of everybody.

Still, it is the innate nature of every living person that we have a certain need to see ourselves, feel ourselves, as being different—somehow . . . special. Many of us work that out through our cultures.

There's the Black culture, Hispanic culture, Jamaican, Native American, Asian. You get the point. Then there's the differences in the color of our skins or of our native tongues.

Again, every single person has this same need to be special.

One way we all go about creating that on this conscious reality side of life is with our idioms of speech. We all have our funny way of talking within our own crowd that goes beyond the common language being spoken.

Black people call it *jive talkin'*. When referring to Liberals, I call it *wokie-tokin'*. You see, we also have come up with a new category of separation called politics—Liberals and Conservatives. As a Conservative, I came up with that term because of the "woke" culture of intolerance exhibited by most Liberals. To me, being *woke* simply means someone who likes to take offense with any ideas or ideals that differ from his or her own.

Why? Now that is the real question plaguing mankind. We all, to some extent, seem to do it. When someone's difference is an actual threat, now that may call for actual action. And unless they have some contagious disease, or we are at war, that threat is almost nonexistent. So, what is the real issue? Why would anyone want to take offense?

Yeeee-ah . . . that would be because of our society—its rules and especially its lies. These aspects of all societies are aimed at who and what we should be and do. That calls for control by society. Those being controlled are always victims.

Yes, ergo the lie. We are trained to see ourselves as victims. Victims are easier to control. It's their natural inclination to follow the rules. As a victim, they don't realize that life—all of it—is a matter of choices. But wouldn't we each make those choices for ourselves *were we not a victim*? Being a victim, life is always on the defense. How better to defend that with offense, as in *taking offense*.

Getting back to the original issue . . . the choice of talking differently to your own crowd, as in jive talkin'. Or as the Hispanics are want to do, throwing some extra-heavy accent and Spanish words like "ese" into the mix. With Liberals, it is in the energy—of making others unacceptable, or less-than, by the superiority of their tone, all the while trying to protect their insecurities by being themselves, on the offense.

Yes, we all have our ways of separating one another, dividing ourselves, making ourselves out to be "better than." It all boils down to the spiritual level and the Spiritual Laws, the simple truths of life. In my own jive redneck lingo, here it is:

We're all just fucking ourselves in holding ourselves as being apart from others—somehow . . . better than.

There is the big kahuna of the Spiritual Laws which states: *I am the Creator.* That means that I create my own life and everything in it—including how I choose to view you. Racism begins not with them, out there, but with me, in here.

Questions:
- How do you, yourself, hold yourself apart from others?
- It is NOT always about being better-than. Maybe it is about being comfortable—as in, not looking within yourself for your answers.
- When looking within, we often see that it is really about making ourselves "right." D'ya think you'd see that if you looked within you?

Actions:
- ➤ Go back over all your answers in your notebook. Those that you answered with a simple "yes" or "no"—ask yourself, why?
- ➤ Was it so you didn't have to look within? Was it so you could simply be "right" without question? Admitting you want to be "better than" is a hard thing to face.
- ➤ Write about that.

We, the Parents—We, the Patriots

How many years of foreign wars has America been involved in and then just walked away? World War II is the last war we finished and actually won.

In fact, it's been some fifty years since the clusterfuck called Vietnam. And those wars have all been fought for monetary gain—for making a lot of very powerful control freaks rich. These days, we know them as "the deep state." They are the ones who are actually controlling we who fight and die in those fucked-up wars. Those who we thought were our actual leaders were simply pawns of the deep state.

Yes, we, the parents, have raised millions of patriot warriors. Until recently, we were the ones who taught them to be patriots, to believe in what this country was said to stand for. We, the true patriots, who believe in the freedoms given by the Creator and spelled out in The Constitution.

It has only recently been that the lying shitbags, now known as the deep state players, have been indoctrinating the children of those patriots into being the tools of their own power . . . teaching them to blindly follow and to disregard all that *We, the Parents* hold dear and true.

And in the meantime, those deep state shitbags have come out of the dark closets and corners where they have always operated from within the halls of government. We are now seeing them in the light of truth, and *We, the Parents, We, the Patriots* are now demanding our promised freedoms back.

Even we, the veterans from that long-ago Vietnam era, many of us can still pull a trigger. I don't think those deep state shitbags realize how big an army they are facing—an army that took a lifelong oath to protect and defend those freedoms The Constitution promises.

Questions:

- Do we have to take it back through force of arms? Unlike other freedom-loving countries—Canada and Australia, for instance—*We, the Parents* are still armed. We still have the power to take back control. Both Australia and Canada do not.
- The deep state fucked up by involving us in all those wars we fought in order to enrich their coffers. By training us to be citizen warriors, they have provided us with the knowledge and ability to take our future freedoms back.
- I expect the shit will fly when they come for our guns. Yes, they will need to use the armed forces, which are made up of our children. Will there be enough of them willing to kill *We, their Parents*?
- I think not. Will it be the beginning of the end of those shitbags—even with all their power and control? Or will it be the end of free societies worldwide? *We, the Parents, We, the Patriots* . . . we are the pivotal point for this whole FUCKING world. Are you AWARE?

Actions:

- ➢ Use common sense and love your children.
- ➢ That may be a hard thing to do if the deep state politicians remain in power. Kick their FUCKING asses out this next election.
- ➢ Indite and press charges. Remove them from society— permanently.
- ➢ Begin with those who would delegitimize our elections. Those we can now prove cheated in the 2020 election would be a good place to start . . . including those who paid them to do it.

Reeks of Politics

The bottom line of Liberalism is power—the control of others. But the truth? *Control is never love. It is always fear. And the bottom line of all fear? It is ALWAYS a cry for love.*

Thing is, a Liberal's power always starts with little stuff. Things that would make your life uncomfortable if you don't do what they want. But the truth is, *others can only have as much control over you as you will allow. This is the law.*

Most people capitulate on the small stuff. Others see it and do so also. They are the sheeple who never see that the demands just get bigger until that Liberal asshole has some considerable influence over everyone (power).

Don't give way on the little stuff. Don't be that first sheeple.

Know the truth. Say the truth. Live the truth. Teach the truth to all the sheeple who will listen.

This is the ONLY war you will need to fight with your designated asshole. Am I engaging in your battle just in telling you the truth of life from the standpoint of the Spiritual Laws—life's simple truths?

Or am I propping up your designated asshole's backbone with that truth so maybe they will understand and let go of their fearful need for power? Will they build your own foundation with the concepts of life that work? With life's truths? They won't if no one shows them.

Yes, we all have our perception. It is what makes up our whole world. Mine works for me. It might also work for you if you could but see it. THAT is the question this book poses to you . . . to all the assholes and sheeple of the world.

Does it bother you to be lumped in with the others just so? Yes, it takes great courage to look at something you don't want to see—especially if that something is pointing a spotlight at one of those mythical things that make you "wrong" . . . where "right" and "wrong" make up the foundation of your own perception.

Don't you get it? This book is not about me clinging to my own mythical "rights." It is merely me sharing some of those truths. So few people ever see them, and fewer still have the courage to accept and live—to build them into the foundation of their lives.

Believe it or not, everything I've written here that reeks of politics was written with love. The "reeking" part is merely that politics ALWAYS reeks of power. Again, you can only have as much power as people will allow. The fact that so many sheeple will allow you ANY power over themselves is what reeks.

Liberal assholes and sheeple? Do you really want to make such a disgusting stink of your life?

The bottom line about politicians? They are always about power. But are there never any leaders.

Questions:
- Can you see that the cornerstones of most "normal" people's lives are the terms "right and wrong" and "good and bad"?
- Don't you think we need to look at that a little closer?

Action:
- Let's do that now.

Here's the Kicker

In the very first entry of the Introduction Section, you were asked to get a notebook for answering the questions and/or doing the actions.

Did you?

If you didn't, then obviously you weren't playing on the field of life, rather only observing the game.

But hey—this isn't a guilt trip. I mean it only so that you might look at your life and see the truth about how yourself. If you want to play in the gameplay in the game, this is your invitation. I suspect it was your soul that picked up this book. If you get another invitation it might be given in an ICU—like mine was.

You were also asked to reserve your answers to the questions and/or the actions to the right-hand sheet of paper. And you were coached to go back after reading this book and answer anything you may have skipped over using the left-hand sheets.

That would be now!

As you are doing this, be aware that many of the questions asked could be answered with a simple YES or NO. That is your soul pointing out your score card in this game of life— HOW you are playing this game. Did you play it to the hilt? Did you add an explanation about HOW anything in your mind was changed? In other words . . .

DID YOU DO YOUR OWN FUCKING THINKING?

If you didn't, now is your chance to go back and do it. The uptake from this will be that you will become aware of exactly how your life has been changed by your thinking.

Change your mind —
Change your whole … fucking … life!

Questions—my wish for you is that your answers will mean as much to you as mine have to me.

- Do you get that *right* and *wrong* and *good* and *bad* don't exist anywhere out there in this whole big fucking world? Not even when punctuated by profanity?
- They only exist in your mind—in your own personal world.
- Don't you think you would do well to remember that those things are just the judgmental titles YOU hang on them?
- They are the shit from between your ears—the part of you that stinks.

Action:
- ➢ Let go of *right* and *wrong* and just see it all as "***what is***".

Epilogue

I've told you some really good shit. Now is the time for fertilizing the garden. And maybe to get out the toilet paper and wipe up some ego. You don't want your ass to be stinky to the rest of humanity, do you?

What this book series is REALLY about is personal power—your innate power to control your personal Universe. It has been termed in many ways, but you are one of the few who is now conscious of it.

"The power of a mustard seed" is how the Christians say it.

Yes, you do have that kind of power, depending on your sense of self. That's right, your ego is a very necessary thing.

Most are never conscious of it. Was Hitler? I dunno. But Jesus? I'm sure Jesus was. We are all a part and piece of God, but God is not "alive"—not as you and I know life. God cannot live this life without you. He/She/It is unable to experience the full scope of life without being able to taste the sweet along with the sour. Only in the realm of life does there exist both. God cannot experience it without incorporating this sentient little YOU. You are the bridge between this world and infinity.

That is why God doesn't give a rat's ass whether you are the sweet part or the sour. AGAIN, isn't it obvious that God's purpose here is to experience life through you?

As for the power of the Universe . . . of God? That power is something YOU possess, as do we all. That mustard seed is merely about our belief in our connection to it all, our sense of "self." In other words, it is the proper use of "ego."

Those who understand this are like a super magnet. They are attractive.

> Some, like Jesus, start religions.
> Some, like Hitler, create chaos.

But YOU personally? YOU are now conscious of it all. And so I urge you to follow some rules. No sane person wants to be another Hitler.

And Jesus? Herding that flock around takes energy that you may not want to expend. After all, it is the energy of your very life.

The rules are simple:

> THE POWER—only use your power to control your own life. And to touch that of others—hopefully with your love.

> THE ENERGY—again, always choose yours to be loving.

> THE INTEGRITY—what you think, what you say, and what you do . . . it all needs to be in alignment.

But keep your mouth shut with humility. That magnetism can take over your whole life.

This series is about personal growth. You are going to stand out in the garden of life. Be as a flower. Don't be a FUCKING weed.

Coach Egorhh

About the Author

In all my books, I talk about an ICU ad nauseam. For me, this life started in one at the age of forty-five. If you are reading this prior to reading the autobiographical novels, an explanation is in order.

You see, before that ICU, I thought my life was full. I came from a working-class family—rednecks, you might say—but my life was not full.

Oh I went places—exciting places—did things, loved, laughed, and generally enjoyed life. I lived a "normal" life.

Lying there with a massive blood clot in my lungs, waiting, fully expecting to die, I could no longer lie to myself. I realized that I'd never really lived.

My early years were spent as the good Mormon son of whom my parents could be proud. Being adopted, that was important to me. But the teachings of the Mormon faith? Well . . . I just never swallowed.

Later, it was as the limp dick, controllable husband my wife demanded. But letting her carry my cojones in her pocket? That was something hard to swallow.

Then there was being that dependable employee my bosses expected while earning my living as a mechanic, a common fender lizard doing a job I hated. All that time was spent being who others wanted. Meanwhile, I never lived the life I wanted.

Hell, I didn't have a clue as to what that life would be like or, in fact, what life in general was about. I lived that façade society demands of all of us, the person we pretend to be in order to be acceptable in the lives of others. Bottom line, I was not someone I could like and respect—or accept. In essence, the phony I was back then did indeed die that day.

There is nothing like facing the Angel of Death to make a person get honest. Facing the truth about myself, I began to see the lies I'd always believed about life . . . the ones adults tell us as children in order to control our lives. Coming as it does from our parents, teachers, religious leaders—everyone in authority—we believed them. We base what we think life is all about upon those lies.

The person I became had vastly different priorities. Most of all, I wanted to become someone I could respect. Facing my fears seemed the place to start. Afraid of heights all my life, I'd regarded myself as a coward. So, I went skydiving.

I also wanted to leave something positive in this world for my life to have mattered. In facing it, I began seeing the lies and realized that I didn't know shit about the truth of life. But I wanted to know. Yes, I then took that "road less traveled" and just naturally fell in beside others, also on that inner journey—the wackos and weirdos, all busy plumbing the depths of the New Age. It wasn't until I discovered "experiential seminars" that I truly dumpster-dived the depths of time and space and learned about New Thought.

By "dumpster," I mean the place where normal folks dump the truth in favor of the lies. And "New Thought"? It's always been around.

You see, New Thought is based on the Spiritual Laws, which are simply what always hold true about life. Ah, but New Thought demands responsibility. You can no longer blame others for anything in your life—especially for your choice in how you feel about it.

For several years, I hung out on the support teams for the seminars. Meanwhile, I took training from We Coach and Coach University. Upon graduating, I then hung up my wrenches and started a Personal Life Coaching practice. That only lasted a few years. While I loved coaching, the hunt for clients was something to be detested. That part seemed to negate the fact that I wanted to be of service to people.

In living life if you worry about what others think of you, you cannot be authentic. And a coach who needs a client more than they need him—same thing. "Authentic" speaks to one's honesty.

That was when I took a job driving paratransit buses, taking disabled people wherever they needed to go. Seeing what they dealt with in their lives was quite a humbling experience. That job satisfied my needs and lasted until I retired.

During those twenty-five years since the ICU, I've been writing about all the wonders I was discovering. Seeing life in the light of the Spiritual Laws—life's great truths—gave me a different perspective.

In attending classes at Community College and hanging out in writer critique groups, I learned the craft of writing. That gave purpose to all I'd learned. Instead of coaching one person at a time, my readers have become my clients. I now write books that coach many people, one book at a time.

My first book, a novel titled *The Courage of a Butterfly*, won a gold literary award. It looks at my earlier life in the light of those truths and showed me quite a different picture. Hopefully, it will illuminate the lives of others as well. The sequel, *The Soul of an Eagle*, outlining my progress through life after that ICU, is now published. In addition, I've published two books of poems that were written into the original manuscripts of those novels.

For more direct coaching, there is this series of four workbooks titled *Redneck Spirituality*—now five. They give an irreverent, in-your-face look at the Spiritual Laws, redneck style.

Most authors writing about Spirituality want their readers to experience the taste of honey and buttercups, to be uplifted and inspired. But the truth of life is that if you want to self-help yourself into making yours better, you've got to look at everything you have spent your lifetime ignoring.

Oh, it will uplift you, but likely, it won't feel good in the doing. That road less traveled can be one bitch of a ride, but the journey is worth every magnificent mile.

One final note:

If you have gleaned any truth from this book series, share it with your loved ones. Populate your world by those with whom you want to share your life. Here, where there are no shepherds or sheeples, where love does not boil down to control and drama but is a true gift requiring no change in who you are, no repayment, and does not expire.

Coach Egorhh